The
HAPPINESS
REVOLUTION

The HAPPINESS REVOLUTION

A MANIFESTO *For* LIVING *Your* BEST LIFE

DR ANDY COPE & PROF PAUL MCGEE

Illustrations by Fiona Osborne

CAPSTONE
A Wiley Brand

REGISTERED OFFICE
John Wiley & Sons Ltd, The Atrium, Southern Gate, Chichester, West Sussex, PO19 8SQ, United Kingdom

For details of our global editorial offices, for customer services and for information about how to apply for permission to reuse the copyright material in this book please see our website at www.wiley.com.

Library of Congress Cataloging-in-Publication Data is Available:

ISBN 9780857088888 (paperback) ISBN 9780857088925 (ePDF)
ISBN 9780857088949 (epub)

Cover Design and Images: Fiona Osborne
Set in 12/16 pt Asap Condensed by Straive, Chennai, India

10 9 8 7 6 5 4 3 2 1

Printed in Great Britain by Bell and Bain Ltd, Glasgow

CONTENTS

Part 1

HAPPINESS, MISSING IN ACTION

Part 2

Part 3

Tales of the Unexpected (and Unexplained)

HAPPINESS,
MISSING IN
ACTION

REVOLUTION
[rev-o-lu-tion]

i Activity or movement designed to effect fundamental changes in the socioeconomic situation

ii A fundamental change in the way of thinking about or visualising something: a change of paradigm

iii The overthrow or repudiation of a regime or political system by the governed

It's almost as if civilisation has become less ... civil.

In this section of the book we look at why happiness has become harder to come by. You'll get a personal invite to the revolution, learn a fabulous Latin phrase, chat to some runner beans and meet some unhappy bunnies.

There's some academic dirty talk and we invite you to choose between two made up diseases: gray brittle death or Hawaiian cat flu.

We also introduce 'change-quakes', and balance out some silly stuff (we take a trip to 2007 in a DeLorean) with serious material (cognitive load theory and the fundamental organising principle of the brain).

All in all, Part 1 goes some way to introducing you to the notion that change in the external world has not been matched by change between your ears. Plot spoiler - basically, the world has outpaced us and we're struggling to keep up.

The first section is concluded with a quick overview of Andy's research. Again, a deliberate light touch to 12 years of hard graft because we figure that you just need the basics, followed by some how-tos.

But first, we're going to ask you to do less and stop trying.

Buckle up. It's gonna get bumpy.

VIVE LA RÉVOLUTION

We hear a lot about the far left
and the far right, but never
the far middle.

The problem with most revolutions is that they can get messy. They're associated with rabble rousing, bloodletting, overthrows and mass demonstrations. People can lose their heads.

This isn't that.

Welcome to our *alternative* revolution.

THE HAPPINESS REVOLUTION is centred on the most sought after 'thing' on the planet. We had to put 'thing' in inverted commas because, technically, happiness isn't a 'thing'. It's not got a shape, form or mass. Happiness is an emotion. A feeling. It's something we want more of for ourselves and if we asked you what you want for your children and grandchildren – and you could only have *ONE* thing – that'd be happiness too. Like us, you're not too bothered about what jobs they end up doing or who they end up marrying (or not), so long as your offspring are happy.

> Happiness, so sought after, so in demand. *Yet so scarce and fleeting.*

We need to come clean at the outset. There are no guarantees. There is no single happiness silver bullet. But we promise you that there are ways and means of improving your chances of having more good days and fewer stinkers.

Rather than waiting (*and waiting and waiting and waiting...*) for evolution to equip us with the necessary skills to thrive, we're inviting you to join a revolution. Don't fret – Paul and myself have no goons or henchmen and we're absolutely NOT asking you to grab a pitchfork and march to Parliament. To avoid any misunderstanding, we're calling it a 'quiet revolution'. An uprising of wellbeing and a raising of the bar from mental health to mental *wealth* because, bottom line, there's a world shortage of happiness right now. In fact, there's a glut of the total opposite, hence our call to action to every person on the planet.

We're pitching in at whatever's the opposite of doomsday and herein lies the nub of the problem. I've just Googled 'doomsday' and there is no opposite. The dictionary gives me 26 disaster synonyms (meltdown, apocalypse, bloodbath, catastrophe and suchlike) but no equivalent good day. It seems the Four Horsemen of the Apocalypse can ride into town unopposed. And that's pretty much what's happened. Negativity has had the upper hand for way too long. We're well versed in phobias and disorders. We have entire systems in place to catch the anxious and unwell. Psychologists have spent 150 years perfecting pills, potions and therapies and yet mental ill health has got staggeringly worse.

> 'Thousands of people are living lives of screaming desperation where they work long hours at jobs they hate to enable them to buy things they don't need to impress people they don't like.'
> [Nigel Marsh]

We understand that when you buy a personal development book, you want some answers. Give me some strategies, ideas and techniques. I need to learn how to wrestle back some control of my life. I want to regain my sanity, clarity and wellbeing. I want to learn how to feel amazing in a world that seems hell bent on knocking me sideways.

I've paid my money, *now tell me how to feel good!*

And because you care, you give said strategies a really good go. You meditate and journal. You're up at 4 am to create your 'miracle morning'.

You become a kindness ninja and a grand master of gratitude. You yoga yourself silly. Diet: *tick*. Sleep hygiene: *tick*. You breathe and smile and work super hard at being positive. You master the power of now. You define your purpose, discover your strengths and get into a flow state. You set goals. You visualise. If you've read *The Secret*, you chant mantras in an effort to 'manifest' things into your life.

And yet...

...the Ferrari never arrives. The nagging doubts remain. Whatever was missing is *still* missing.

David Hare describes it as painting over the rust.

> **We're really good at applying glossy new wellbeing techniques upon the rustiest girder of discontentment and exhaustion.**

We can have the very best intentions, but it doesn't take long for the rust to bubble through. Rather than glossing over bad habits, true personal development needs to take some sandpaper to the rustiness.

> **So here's our deal; it's time to try *less* hard.**

I know! It doesn't seem right to die and leave the world in a mess – but everybody does it, so chill. You can't cure the world. Caring with a passion is noble and well intentioned, but it will also make your knees buckle. Instead, why not treat yourself to some 'subtractive psychology'. Jettison some responsibility. Shed some thinking. Let go of tired old habits. Park your negativity. Drop the guilt. Offload that nagging self-doubt. With that excess baggage gone, the spring returns to your step, a smile to your face and, bizarrely, the world becomes much more doable.

Our book has a touch of the counter-intuitives about it. Our advice is to look around at what everyone else is doing and NOT do that! In a world where we've already got enough to do, it's our belief that the solution is not only to try less hard, but also to do less.

Do less, but *be* more.

Humanity has somehow managed to worry itself sick. In which case we think it must be perfectly possible to *un-worry yourself well*. Let the good times roll. Quite simply, we want you to sign up to being your best self. *Consistently*. And while that might not change THE world, it'll certainly shape yours.

So what does an uprising of wellbeing look like?

The truth is that nobody really knows.

Nobody is ever described as 'stark raving happy'.

The news never reports on a bunch of smilers who are so overjoyed with life that they've made placards and have organised a demonstration and a march to parliament to proclaim their satisfaction with life. There's never an announcement that 'This hospital is working so brilliantly that we've instigated an independent review to look at the evidence to find out why it's so epic'.

The mass celebration of wellbeing has to start somewhere, and we're suggesting the best place is with you. No petitions, pitchforks, placards, protest marches or toppling of statues required. This revolution is so quiet that nobody will hear it because it takes place in your head. But, my goodness, they'll see it alright.

Because once you sort things out between your ears, it shows in your behaviours, which ripple out into your loved ones and beyond.

You become an example of what an awesome human being looks, sounds and feels like. Yes, dearest reader, we're asking you to join a revolution that feeds into a worldwide movement. It's our cunning plot to take over the world. In an era of rising anxiety, panic and tumult, it's time to make a stand – to become one of the few rather than one of the many. ~~Let's fight them on the beaches, let's fight on the landing grounds, let's fight in the fields and in the streets…~~

Sorry, wrong speech.

Let the fight back to mental wealth start right here. Welcome to global domination of the *happiness* kind.

Mwah ha ha ha haaaaaa!

A brand new beginning. That's where the revolution starts. We'd therefore like to raise a glass and propose a simple toast:

To you. Welcome home. Welcome back to your best self.

You Are Cordially Invited To Join

The

HAPPINESS
REVOLUTION

When: Right Now **Where:** Right Here

What to bring: Come as you are
(dancing shoes will be required)
Bring a like-minded friend

Directions: Read the book. Apply the learning

RSVP to: ✳HappinessRevolution

LEARN LATIN

SEMPER IN
FAECIBUS
SUMUM, SOLE
PROFUNDUM
VARIAT

It feels lovely to bag a bargain. Consumers are drawn in by '25% off', tempted by '30% extra free' and we don't half love a meal deal. My cupboards are filled with tins of red kidney beans, plundered in last month's 3 for 2 supermarket sweep. When the apocalypse comes, our household is ready.

While 'buy one get one free' is common in the kidney bean and biscuit aisle, it's less common with writing. And yet here we are. Congratulations, you bagged yourself a *two authors for the price of one* mega deal.

We're hugely excited to have you aboard. Truthfully, we're beyond excited. We're honoured. So as a big fat 'THANK YOU' we thought we'd be the bearers of good news. If you're reading this book, there are two immediate stand-out plus points: first, congratulations, *you're alive*. And second, *you can read*. That's two huge reasons to smile, and we haven't even started yet!

We've written **THE HAPPINESS REVOLUTION** to give you a breather from the human race, a deliberate time out to help you catch your breath. Our third piece of superb news is that you can chill.

The chase for happiness is over. We've called off the dogs. It's time to build a life that you don't need to escape from.

Before the revolution swings into action, a quick note about content, style and what to expect. Your two for one author deal is good value for the readers but presents a challenge for the writers. A 'whose line is it anyway?' identity challenge. We've thought long and hard about the best way to overcome this writing conundrum. Then longer and harder before coming to the conclusion that it doesn't matter. Not a jot.

The world has shifted, shaping the English language with it. With fluidity comes a choice of preferred personal pronouns – she, he, they, their, ze, zie (there are plenty more in the modern lexicon) – so we're choosing to ask you to *not care*.

Please think of us as one voice. Even when we say 'I', we're actually a 'we'.

As for who 'we' are, that doesn't matter a great deal either. Sure, Paul's a professor of something or other and Andy's a doctor of the counterintuitive. There's a solid academic background. Basically, we've ploughed through the academic papers so you don't have to.

But **THE HAPPINESS REVOLUTION** isn't really about that.

Your *buy one get one free* author tag team, we've been there done that, made mistakes and learned heaps along the way. We've got a combined 100+ years of being alive, 60 years of marriage, 50 years of parenting, 30 years of running our businesses and a back catalogue of 20 or so books. We have grey hairs to prove it. We've had gritty life experience, some success, some serious screw-ups and we're both riddled with character flaws. We're far from perfetc.

THE HAPPINESS REVOLUTION absolutely *is* about that.

The reason we're still here, still standing, is based on much of what you're about to read.

It's taken us years to learn this stuff, and more importantly to apply it to our own lives. So, by all means check out the science and the theories behind what we write, but read with your heart, not just your head. Read to be inspired and entertained, rather than simply informed. I don't think either of us just want to titillate your mind. We'd rather cleanse your palate, refresh your thinking, and reenergise your spirit in preparation for whatever life throws at you.

It won't have escaped your notice that life is capable of throwing a lot! The Latin phrase *Semper in faecibus sumum, sole profundum variat* sums up the current state of play... *we're always in the shit, it's just the depth that varies.*

Right now, we're up to our necks.

Generally speaking, our back catalogue of personal development books has focused on how to maximise possibilities and fulfil our potential. This book also seeks to do exactly that. The difference is we're starting with an acknowledgement that the world has been doing its worst lately.

> **Life has always been a contact sport but recently it's gotten brutal.**

It's become like the best World Wrestling Federation bout ever; with the referee distracted, life is able to smash a chair across your head, leaving you staggering around in your pants.

How did we end up so bewildered? We've more money than ever before and more access to life-enhancing stuff to make our lives easier and more comfortable. And yet we're popping more pills, and tragically cutting our lives short in record numbers.

It's heartbreaking.

> **We want to make sure those pains and problems don't become permanent and pervasive.**

The hand-me-down beliefs and behaviours we received from our parents haven't equipped us to compete well in the game of life. The game used to be so simple and now, more likely, your life has some amazing characters but you're struggling to work out the plot?

Call it a lucky guess!

Both of your authors are keynote speakers, which means we get the same questions asked of us. We thought it'd be worth ticking off two biggies upfront.

First, can you deliver something that's 'evidence based'?

Understandably, what people are asking for is something that's provable. Whoever's organising the conference wants a speaker with credibility so something grounded in science would go down well. Sure thing. Both the Prof and Doc can give you some content that's got science behind it. We'll provide academic references where necessary.

Evidence based is good, but we're more interested in **THE HAPPINESS REVOLUTION** being *truth* based, the truth being that our version of science might not sound like science. The absolute truth is that after gaining a PhD in human flourishing, I haven't learned anything that I didn't already know before I started. Sure, I can wrap it up to make it sound sciencey, something I describe as academic porn – *'Gosh what a big brain you've got. Use those big words on me baby. Remind me of the T-Tests results for respondents on the 16 emotions measured by the IWP Multi-Affect Indicator that you discuss in your PhD thesis. Whisper those sweet findings into my ear. Let me have your Chi-squared stats and your p-values. Give them to me hard…'*

Dearest reader, you'll not find that kind of academic filth in this book. Paul and I don't speak like that and, quite frankly, we prefer to write how we speak.

Life's got heavy, so we've *deliberately* decided to go light. The italics is important. Our lightness of touch opens us up to criticism from the sesquipedalians. [Those who prefer big words. I mean, who knew?]. It's

easy to accuse us of dumbing down when, in truth, the aim is to simplify. That sentence is bigger than it sounds.

**We're seeking to communicate in a way that is relevant,
to give knowledge that is do-able and to be entertaining
enough to keep the pages turning.**

However, please don't mistake our light touch for light content.
THE HAPPINESS REVOLUTION is partly a book about surviving, because
that's where some people are at present, but it is also a book about
thriving. Thriving in our relationship with ourselves and with others
whilst recognising that conflict, challenge, setbacks and disappointments are part of the journey. If you drill into its DNA you'll find
THE HAPPINESS REVOLUTION is about resilience, responsibility, kindness and compassion.

The second very common question in the training world is, can you do
a talk for a specific group of people? So, for example, can you run a
workshop for maths teachers? Or, we've got some engineers who need
pepping up. Or, we've got a cohort of 16 year olds who need to raise
their aspirations. Or, we've got a nurses' conference, can you design
a talk specifically for them? . . .

My answer is that I can make it *sound* as though it's specifically for
them, so if it's a talk for teachers, I can mention the word 'teacher'
a lot. But it's not really about that. Teaching, nursing, engineering,
these are part-time jobs.

**Your full-time occupation is 'human being', so we're keen
to make our message fit across all the domains of your life.**

With that in mind, we've written **THE HAPPINESS REVOLUTION** with a very specific audience in mind: if you fall into the category of 'human being' we sincerely hope you enjoy this book. We've written it *especially* for you.

WATERING YOUR WEEDS

We call my wife 'the plant whisperer'. She's very handy with a trowel and a bag of manure and can literally coax lettuce from between the paving stones of our patio. I followed her around our vegetable patch one time, watching, learning and listening to her whisperings.

She was so encouraging of the courgettes; *'You guys are doing so well. I'm so proud of how far you've come.'* She slipped them a slug pellet, almost surreptitiously, as though it was a banned substance. *'And this'll help you grow even bigger.'*

She clapped her hands in glee at the runner beans. *'Oh my giddy aunt, just look at you little rascals, all tall and slender and handsome.'*

Is it right that I felt a twinge of jealousy? About runner beans?

But the plant whisperer is not all sweetness and light. The cabbages got a right telling off; *'You lazy things. You should be ashamed of your-selves. You've really let yourselves go this year.'*

Then we came across a rather sad and forlorn-looking rose bush, and the plant whisperer stopped in her tracks, sniffed one of the half-open buds and her face fell. *'Well you're not a happy bunny.'* I'm no expert but I'm assuming 'bunny' was the Latin term for that particular rose.

While I admit to not knowing my dahlias from my marigolds, I do know the ins and outs of personal development and *'not a happy bunny'* put me in mind of Carol Dweck's fixed and growth mindsets.[1] This is common language in schools but in case you're not familiar, let me remind you of the basics. Dweck conducted research on hundreds of 11 year olds in which she set a series of puzzles at the end of which she gave them scores and praise. Half were given praise which suggested they were gifted and talented, hence she used phrases along the lines of 'you are so smart at this'. The others were given praise that reflected the effort they'd put in, so for example; 'you must have worked really hard'.

Then, in what sounds like an experiment in child cruelty, she gave them another test – a much sterner test – in fact so tough it was impossible. Of course, none of the kids did very well but she discovered that those who'd been given praise for their intelligence soon capitulated.

[1] Dweck, C. S. (2006). *Mindset: The New Psychology of Success.* New York: Random House.

It's as though they'd decided, en masse, they weren't so clever after all, whereas those who were praised for effort did 'a Billy Ocean' (my words not Professor Dweck's). Basically, when the going got tough, these 'growth mindset kids' got going. Against the odds, they improved their scores by 30%.

Academia works on a whack-a-mole principle, so no matter how in vogue your theory, someone with a bigger forehead will eventually peer review your work, pick it to bits and propose their own 'new improved theory'. That's how knowledge inches forward. Hence Dweck's ideas have been kicked from pillar to post but sometimes it's best to ignore the noise and focus on the main point. You don't need a PhD in anything to see that Dweck's basic principle holds water. A top tip that arises directly from her work is simply to praise your children for effort rather than talent.

But what's this got to do with my wife's roses? The 'not a happy bunny' comment reflected that the plant was not growing. It was trying hard enough but for some reason the rose wasn't flourishing and its buds didn't look like they would blossom. We had no desire to bend down and smell its fragrance. It was taking up space in our borders, but even I could tell it wasn't growing in the way roses are meant to grow.

Dweck talks about dandelion and orchid characters. If you have a garden, you'll notice that dandelions are hardy and perennial. Basically, they crop up everywhere. They don't require watering or feeding. You can mow them and they're back in a day or two, shrugging off the recent beheading calamity, their yellowness tilting towards the sun. Orchids on the other hand… if you've ever tried to get one to bloom you'll appreciate that it requires a lot of love, effort and a wheelbarrow full of luck. Orchids require perfect soil conditions, just the right amount of feeding, a Goldilocks amount of sunshine and, even then, they might only bloom for a day or two.

The point is that some humans are like dandelions. They just seem to flourish in whatever situation/job/environment you put them in. Knock 'em down and they spring back up. But most of us (and by 'us' we include the majority of readers and both your authors) are trying our best to bloom in an environment that's against us. And when we do bloom, it's a quick blast of wonderfulness, and then our petals drop.

You see, unlike when buying a plant, we don't come with a small plastic card highlighting when to prune and water us, and how much sunshine we prefer. Nope, we enter this world naked, screaming, and solely reliant on people who would have more background checks made on them if they were adopting a cat than bringing a human life into the world.

Whatever upbringing we have and whatever environment we find ourselves in, we do our best to flourish. We fight off being strangled by the weeds of negativity and we do our best to stand tall when the world does its worst. The shifting seasons are a reminder that nothing's designed to bloom all the time. It's a blessed relief to know that even Mother Nature has down time where she rests and replenishes.

We all understand the mantra: it's okay NOT to be okay. But there are times when 'not a happy bunny' doesn't do justice to the depth of our despair. If we're continually being pruned and mowed and flooded there may come a time when the unhappy bunny really starts to struggle. So before we go any further, it's worth pausing to reflect on those times. The COVID-19 pandemic blighted the lives of millions but it's small fry in comparison to the *billions* who've been affected by the pandemic of mental illness.

The mental *ill*-health statistics are staggering. We'll spare you the details and just scare you with the headlines. The rise and rise of the problem is hard to plot exactly. It's a recent phenomenon that the medical profession has been tracking for a couple of decades, but go back any further than that and mental health wasn't deemed serious enough to warrant any gathering of data. A rough trawl of the research hints that pre-World War I about 1 in 10,000 people suffered from one of the various mental illnesses. PTSD or 'shell shock' took its toll and post-World War II, it was 1 in 100. In the 1980s, about 1 in 20 people suffered some form of diagnosable wellbeing disorder and by the early 21st century it was 1 in 4.[2]

Today? In any given year almost 30 per cent of the adult population will suffer from a recognised psychological disorder. The World Health Organization has recently stated that depression is now the biggest, costliest, and most debilitating disease in the world.[3]

From a standing start to a crippling mental health pandemic in the space of three generations. If you extrapolate the figures, by 2050 it will be unusual NOT to have some sort of diagnosable mental health disorder and by 2080 almost everyone will be suffering.

This book aims to help you find the pot of happiness gold at the end of the rainbow, but we can't ignore the fact that the emotional spectrum has a dark side. If you go to the depression end of the rainbow you'll find no sunshine and instead of a pot of gold, there's a black dog with no wag. There is a spectrum, with colours ranging from light grey, to darker grey to even darker grey and noir. The gloom feels pervasive and permanent. When happiness is extinguished, hope goes with it.

---

[2] For an overview read The History of Mental Health Services in Modern England: Practitioner Memories and the Direction of Future Research. https://www.ncbi.nlm.nih.gov/pmc/articles/PMC4595954/

[3] 'Depression: let's talk' says WHO, as depression tops list of causes of ill health. https://www.who.int/news/item/30-03-2017--depression-let-s-talk-says-who-as-depression-tops-list-of-causes-of-ill-health

Your past seems dark, your present bleak and your future appears as monotonous grey pointlessness.

Your author tag team are in the same corner as Russ Harris[4] (author of *The Happiness Trap*) who couldn't be any clearer when he says that having a depressive disorder is NOT:

- **Being sad about a bad situation**
- **Grieving the loss of a loved one**
- **All in a person's head**
- **Overreacting or being over emotional**
- **Something that a person just 'gets over'**
- **A pity party**
- **Being stuck in a rut**
- **Laziness**
- **A choice**
- **A sign of weakness**
- **A character flaw**

There's a saying that pain is inevitable but suffering is optional. The first half is bang on. It's nailed on that everyone will get ill, lose loved ones, experience relationship breakups, have arguments, lose their job, miss out on a promotion and work their way through pandemics.

[4] Harris, Russ (2008). *The Happiness Trap: Stop Struggling, Start Living*. London: Robinson Publishing.

But what about the second half of the sentence – *suffering is optional?* That might be true if you're a cold, emotionless psychopath. but for the majority of us suffering isn't something we can take or leave. We suffer because we care. It's built into the fabric of our lives. Suffering is a recurring theme.

There are plenty of plausible explanations for the rise and rise of worry, anxiety, panic, self-harm and suicide. Devil's advocate, just for a second, it could be that we've been birthing a batch of faulty human beings. Like a 1970s British Leyland production line, we've got a batch who are prone to breaking down. Everyone's heard of the 'snowflake' generation but the only way to test it would be to transplant your average person from 1767 and plonk them in today's hurly burly world, and track how they get on. Would they be tougher and more resilient? Would they cope just fine?

Would they heck! Give them 300 emails to sort before lunchtime, introduce them to social media, get them to pay for parking on an app, book and catch a train from Tamworth to Euston, attend an online meeting and explain microwave meals to them. Day one, their heads would explode.

Which leaves us with the prospect that if humans haven't changed, there must be something in the environment that's causing us to go haywire.

It's not us that's changed, it's that our environment has become more toxic.

Let's take that hypothesis as our starting point.

ALL ABOARD
THE
STRUGGLE BUS

'For a long time it had seemed to me
that life was about to begin – real life.
But there was always some obstacle in the
way, something to be gotten through first,
some unfinished business, time still to
be served, a debt to be paid. Then life
would begin. At last it dawned on me
that these obstacles were my life.'

[Alfred D. Souza.
Not entirely sure who he was,
but his words ring true]

Depending on which clever researchers, anthropologists and demographers you believe, the best guess is that over 100 billion humans have lived on planet earth over the last 200,000 years. Of those hundred billion people, just short of eight billion are currently alive now.

Picture it like the London Marathon, but with eight billion runners. I'm with the TV crew in the helicopter. I can see you down there, dressed as a superhero, jostling for position in the human race.

Go you!

Just do this little exercise with me.

Whatever your age, go back to 9 months before you were born. In my case, that takes us back to the heady days of mid-November 1963, around the time President Kennedy was shot and 'Surfin' USA' was riding high in the charts.

Now I'll spare you the gory details but I'm guessing that, like me, you were born as a result of two people having a moment of intimacy (and I realise that the word 'moment' could be anything from a few seconds to a full minute) and with any luck you were born approximately 40 weeks later. Although some of you were so keen to announce your arrival to the world that you decided to make your entrance earlier, whilst if you were like me you felt rather comfortable floating around in a sack of amniotic fluid, sucking your thumb and needed to be yanked out of your state of peaceful bliss with the help of some rather vicious looking metal instrument which you'd normally see being used to flip burgers on a BBQ.

Either way, that moment of intimacy months previously ultimately led to a miracle. You.

Yep, I use the word 'miracle' deliberately. You see, drawing on my extensive academic background in biology (CSE grade 3 in 1980) I have been able to ascertain that the actual chances of you being born with your own specific set of genes and chromosomes was well over a squillion to one. That father of yours released a significant amount of sperm – but only one little fella won the race to fertilise your mum's egg.

You were the champion front-crawler, wriggler or breast-stroker (excuse the pun).

And despite the fact that over 100 billion *Homo sapiens* have populated the planet over the last 200,000 years, there's never been anyone quite like you. Your DNA is unique. That's why your saliva on the murder victim is never good news. You are made of 37 trillion cells,[1] each one containing the same DNA, the blueprint of you. Your height, eye colour, basic body shape, shoe size . . . these are pre-determined.

But the brand new science of epigenetics suggests the *sequencing* of your genes is dependent largely on your environment. Your genes can be switched on and off. That means you are moulded by experiences.

Genes load the gun. Your behaviour and environment pull the trigger.

[1] https://www.smithsonianmag.com/smart-news/there-are-372-trillion-cells-in-your-body-4941473/

Let me choose a disturbing example so you'll remember it. An abused child will be experiencing extreme stress. The body's response is to switch on the cortisol tap and douse your body with hormones that will enable you to deal with adversity. The child becomes primed for fight or flight. When the child is rescued from their terrible upbringing, the cortisol hose remains switched on, hence the adult is in fight or flight mode for the rest of their lives. Always jumpy, never able to settle, lacking trust in others and always struggling to form strong loving relationships. Basically, the environment has altered the genetic sequencing of that human being. I can't make it any clearer than this: they were born fine and the world has screwed them up.

The good news is that epigenetics also works the other way. If you're brought up in a loving environment, oxytocin washes around your body which, I promise you, is a lot healthier. You feel safe, so you explore your potential, take calculated risks, make good decisions and are better able to create strong bonds with family, friends and work colleagues.

The point being that it's the same child, with the same DNA. The difference is the environment.

So let's take a look at the external environment and how it might be shaping us right now.

Every single one of the previous 92 billion inhabitants faced challenges of survival. Remember, old age used to be mid-30s. If you could avoid being eaten by predators or other tribes, you were doing well. Disease, starvation, war or a bad winter and BOOM, your entire community would be decimated. I'm talking about humans in year zero. People living in this era were thankful for early technology (fire, the wheel and sharp edges) but there would have been no discernible changes in their lifetime.

If we likened change to an earthquake Richter scale, it was as flat as we thought the earth was. Sure, there was an occasional ripple of locusts, plagues, flood and famine but if you measured 'global change' on the Richter scale the needle would look something like the picture below; centuries of nothingness punctuated by an occasional shock of change.

Let's call it a 'placid' environment.

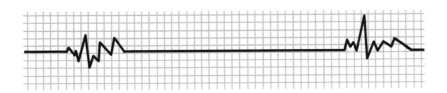

Thankfully, *Homo sapiens* are resourceful creatures. Adversity made us stronger. When the harvest failed to show up, and with 70% of the village wiped out, we'd pick ourselves up, pray to the Gods, sacrifice our first born and start again, but this time with a better drainage system.

The challenges have shapeshifted throughout the ages, but they've always been there. Please excuse the bluntness of my historical summary but if we fast-forward to more modern times, the 19th century brought a revolution of industry. Mass rural–urban migration, the creation of huge cities, breakthroughs in agriculture; the pace of change picked up.

The Richter scale oscillations of change became bigger and more frequent. The periods of nothingness were shorter and when the changes came they were bigger. People could observe changes within their lifetime. Global and local change started to look and feel more like this.

I'm calling it the 'pre-shock' era.

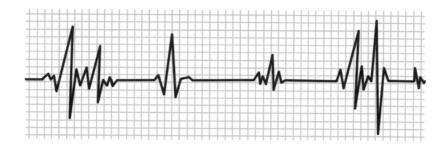

Then along came the 20th century, an era of belching factories and children up chimneys. The acceleration of industrialisation was slowed by two world wars but things settled down and from the 1950s onwards we enjoyed modern housing, central heating, motor cars, commercial flights, foreign holidays, indoor toilets and pizza.

Towards the end of the 20th century technology showed up, big time, in industry and at home. Laughable now, but anyone who can remember a Commodore 64 or a Sinclair ZX80 was at the birth of the tech revolution. As a teenager our school had one computer, a satisfyingly large BBC Micro, that we were able to look at but nobody ever used because nobody knew how.

The Motorola cell phone, circa 1985, neither smart nor mobile, was the starting pistol for an acceleration of the technological race that spilled over into the human race. Our sedentary existence morphed into an exhausting lung-busting lifetime sprint. The epidemic of busyness took hold like a junkyard dog, sinking its teeth into our human hides and refusing to let go. The aim of the 20th century race seemed to be who could accumulate the most stuff.

Already puffed out, we dodged the Millennium Bug and entered the 21st century. The overwhelm that we *thought* we had been experiencing turned out to have just been 'whelm'. In the first two decades of the new millennium we had the kitchen sink thrown at us. The 2020/21 pandemic hurled the fridge, cooker, microwave and a whole load of pots and pans.

Everything got ramped up. The Richter scale needle went bananas. I'm calling it the 'change-quake' zone (think 'twilight zone', but a whole lot scarier).

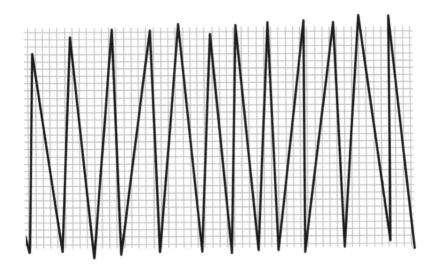

Moore was proven right, his Law of Accelerating Technology[2] left us playing catch-up. Today, ramped up to 5G (and counting) life is moving at cheek-wobbling speed. 'Not happy bunnies' isn't the half of it. It's not just the ever thicker and faster change, it's the lack of downtime between the oscillations. With ears drooping and loss of bounce, a lot of unhappy bunnies are caught in the headlights of modernity. If they're not careful, Flopsy, Mopsy and Cottontail can find themselves flattened by the oncoming rage of the machine.

[2] https://en.wikipedia.org/wiki/Moore%27s_law

'Alexa, how do I cure my addiction to modern technology?'

Please excuse our hyperbole. We are not describing the apocalypse. None of this is necessarily bad. Our standards of living remain astonishingly high. Those in the west are living lifestyles as lavish as kings and queens of yesteryear. Our point is simply that the previous 92 billion custodians of earth never faced the unprecedented oscillations of change that the current eight billion souls face now. It's not a question of 'You've never had it so good', more a case of 'you've never had it so fast, complex and unpredictable'. We're literally making it up as we go along which means some (not all) of the lessons from the past are no longer relevant to right now.

You've got to ignore the craziness around you, in order to deal with the craziness within you.

The problem isn't change *per se*. It's that we've gone from incremental change that would be undetectable in a single lifetime, to 5G-force change that's detectable in a single year, month, week or sometimes even a single day. For example, 20 March 2020, we're all busy at work. 21 March 2020, pandemic pandemonium, *nobody's* at work.

Sure, the COVID pandemic was a cliff edge change whereas most is detectable only through the hue of rose-tinted 'good old days' spectacles. For example, cast your mind back to the recent past. In fact, let's bundle you into a DeLorean and set the timer for 28 June 2007, at, say, 10.37 am. Spark the flux capacitor and away you go, stepping out into a wonderful summer's day. Good news, you're in a parking space and because it's 2007 the machine is simple. There's no app to download. No credit card details to register, no recorded voice recognition system to swear at. It's not a 10-minute job, it's 10 seconds… coin in, ticket out, fixed to your windscreen.

Now where?

Right there, across the road, is a café. As you walk in be sure to survey the scene. The eatery is full of people tucking into their crumpets and coffee but look at the blackboard. How weird, just two or three choices of coffee and, even weirder, people are paying with cash. Check out the locals. Some are reading a newspaper (yes, they were finding out about world events by reading something written yesterday, printed on paper) but here's the startling bit, most are actually deep in conversation with the person they came with.

In the corner you spot one guy on his phone – and this detail is important – which he is holding up to his ear and is clearly *talking* to someone. No one is scrolling. Remember, it's 2007. Screens are for looking at, not swiping. By today's standards, there's an unnerving amount of eye contact and hubbub.

Sound familiar? Probably not. Trust us, though, that's the scene you would have witnessed in that café in the not-so-distant past. How can we be sure? Because although tech was ramping up, it remained fairly pedestrian. Social media was still in 'Friends Reunited' mode. Remember that? It was an actual thing, proof that social media used to be, well, *social!* It's wasn't about trolls, abuse, spitting bile or collecting legions of likes and followers, it was about connecting up with long lost chums from school. That's probably who you're sitting amongst in the 2007 café right now, people reunited after 25 years. Cast your mind back. Wasn't social media wonderful? And innocent.

We sent you back to 2007 for a reason. There was no Instagram, WhatsApp (in fact no apps at all), Snapchat or emojis, and if you wanted to use Facebook or Twitter you had to do so via a laptop or computer.

We chose 28 June for a very specific reason – it's not until *tomorrow* that Steve Jobs launches the iPhone.

PRESUMED GUILTY

Life has given us the ultimate paradox – in a world of abundance, there remains a nagging feeling of emptiness.

The modern world has bent over backwards to give us what we *thought* we wanted – and yet it has somehow driven a wedge between us and happiness. Our relationship with happiness has become strained and, in some cases, annulled. It's not unusual to feel 'divorced' from your mental health. Like a difficult marriage breakup, you might get custody of happiness every other weekend. If you're super-lucky you might get access to happiness for a whole week in the summer.

We are, as the poet Lucretius put it a few thousand years ago, the proverbial 'sick man ignorant of the cause of his malady'. Humans are okay with change. It's what we've always done and we're actually quite good at it. Evolving change, that is. Plodding change. We're even okay with short-term cataclysmic change. But we're not equipped to deal with the speed and magnitude of the ever-present Richter scale 9.6 that's been ripping through society for the last decade or so. The evolution of that magnificent machine we call 'the brain' means

we're still better equipped to deal with woolly mammoths and sabre tooth tigers than we are to juggle an important online meeting, a crying baby and an Amazon delivery.

It's a wiring issue. Two pieces of academia point the way. Reif's cognitive load theory[1] fits the bill. If you simplify it (otherwise you fall foul of the supreme irony that the cognitive load of trying to understand cognitive load theory causes your brain to crash) CLT is about the mental effort of trying to process whatever's on your plate. The point being that if the cognitive load exceeds our processing capacity, we're heading for trouble.

Guess what. We don't have enough mental bandwidth. Our eyes are bigger than our bellies. We're like Oliver. We rather innocently asked, 'Please sir, can I have some more?' and boy, did we get more! More choice, more data, more speed, more pressure, more to do, more complexity, more to match up to, more to catch up with, more to compare with...

...more than we bargained for.

---

[1] Reif, F. (2010). *Applying Cognitive Science to Education. Thinking and Learning in Scientific and Other Complex Domains.* Cambridge, MA: The MIT Press.

> *'The more we have on our mind,
> the more we're prone to behave
> like a bit of a mor(e)on.'*
> **[Michael Neill]**

The second wiring issue is that we have caution baked into our operating system. It's not something you can do a great deal about, other than recognise that's how *Homo sapiens* are manufactured. Psychologists call it negativity bias[2]; it's why you remember criticism and forget a compliment. An awareness of it helps you compensate for it.

Essentially, we didn't evolve for happiness.

Primitive humans didn't sit around journaling or meditating, they were too busy surviving. Our minds evolved to help us survive in a world fraught with danger.

Imagine that you're an early human hunter–gatherer. You have what Stephen Pinker[3] calls the four basic needs, his 4 Fs of feeding, fighting, fleeing and fucking, but none of these things matter if you're dead. So the number-one priority of the primitive human brain was to look out for anything that might harm you – and keep well away. Dr Evian Gordon calls it the 'fundamental organising principle of the brain',

---

[2] Explained rather wonderfully in Haidt, J. (2006). *The Happiness Hypothesis – Putting Ancient Wisdom to the Test of Modern Science.* London: Random House/Arrow.
[3] Pinker, S. (2008). *The Stuff of Thought: Language as a Window into Human Nature.* New York: Penguin.

suggesting our senses scan the environment five times a second, looking for danger.[4]

Five times a *second!*

Basically, humans have an ultra-vigilant 'don't get killed' device, fitted as standard. To be fair, other than those bestowed with a posthumous Darwin Award (worth a Google), our 'don't get killed' radar has served that purpose pretty darned well.

But its hair-trigger reaction speed remains oh so basic. It works on the opposite of the judiciary system – everything and everyone is presumed guilty. If your brain sniffs danger, it's programmed to assume the threat is real unless it can be proved otherwise. In the courtroom, this super cautious 'guilty until proved innocent' mantra would mean a 10-year prison sentence for illegal parking. *Just in case. Because you can never be too careful! A parking fine today could be the start of a murderous spree.*

Caution is **EVERYTHING**! Why? Because back in the fur skin, campfire, axe wielding days, the assumption of clear and present danger saved our bacon. We were programmed to flee from the rustle in the bushes *every single time*, even when it was only a squirrel. This 'better safe than sorry' mechanism means getting it wrong 1000 times and fleeing from 1000 squirrels is better than misjudging it once.

One miscalculation, *one* lapse, *one* moment of carelessness, *one* moment of letting your guard down – it's a bear rather than a squirrel – and you're not bringing home the bacon, you *are* the bacon.

....
[4] Gordon Evian (2000). *Integrative Neuroscience: Bringing Together Biological, Psychological and Clinical Models of the Human Brain*. Boca Raton, FL: CRC Press.

Then, in the blink of an evolutionary eye, we find ourselves slap bang in the 21st century. It's a 5G world and yet our brains are stuck with the same 0.5G operating system. The five-times-a-second rule still applies. We're scanning: is this good or bad, safe or dangerous, harmful or helpful? These days, though, with fewer bears to fret about our minds go to extraordinary lengths to spot dangers elsewhere. We can't help it!

What if I lose my job, can't find a parking space, embarrass myself in a meeting, get cancer, say the wrong thing, take a wrong turn, arrive late or accidentally upset someone on Twitter? What if my mum's dementia gets worse, what if my kids get bullied, does my bum look big in this, is this mole normal…?

> **Our brain becomes the equivalent of an oversensitive smoke alarm that is not only activated by a serious threat – the kitchen is on fire – but also by the equivalent of slightly overdone toast.**

Remember, your mind thinks this is helpful. It's trying to do you a favour, look after you, protect you from harm, save your skin. As a result we spend a lot of time gripped in a double whammy of worrying about things that, more often than not, (a) aren't worth worrying about and (b) will most probably not even happen.

In this light, mental suffering is absolutely not seen as a weakness and most certainly not an illness. It's not the product of a mind that is somehow faulty or defective. It's not that our serotonin switch is faulty.

You're not defective. You're functioning superbly! If you're feeling anxious, congratulations! Your mind's doing exactly what it evolved to do.

The likelihood is, if you're like most other humans on the planet, you've already spent a lot of time and effort trying to have more 'good' feelings and fewer 'bad' ones. You'll have strategies and sometimes they'll work. But it's always a struggle because you're battling against your own human nature.

Yet we are powerless to cease this mental self-harm. Remember, it's baked in. You cannot **NOT** do it.

Hang in there – good news is coming, but first we have to layer on the truth. Back to our Richter scale analogy, while we're lucky to have avoided actual earthquakes, we've been experiencing 21st-century 'change-quakes' and their associated aftershocks. It's not surprising that mental health has nosedived. The surprising fact is that there's anyone left with their wellbeing intact!

There's no prospect of the needle of change calming itself. The 'new normal' has gatecrashed into our lives like an unwelcome house guest. Sticking your fingers in your ears, closing your eyes and shouting '*blah blah blah*' will drown it out temporarily, but when you open your eyes, the noisy shyster will still be there.

There's really only one viable long-term strategy – to learn to be the kind of person who thrives in an uncertain world. Someone who embraces change, who has an ability to bounce back and enough courage to stick a middle finger up to the world when it does its absolute worst.

A 9.6 change-quake? *Bring. It. On!*

Good news, at last! It's possible to learn to be that kind of person. You'd just need to know how. And the best place to start is to take a peek under the bonnet.

NEW TRICKS

'He has well and truly earned his place among our community's outstanding non-achievers.' An easy award to win. Worth trying super-hard NOT to collect this accolade.

For those old enough to remember, think of this section as a Haynes manual for the human being. To understand your wiring, we need to lift the hood. If we took a circular saw to the top of your skull and had a peep inside… there'd be a sharp electrician's intake of breath: 'Sheesh, that's messy. This rewiring project is gonna be a big job.'

Question. Are you born perfect or is it all downhill as soon as you emerge from the birth canal?

> **Most of us suck in our first lungful of oxygen, take a look at our parents and burst into tears.**

Maybe that's a clue, right there?

Anyhow, our question starter is this: are you born a mini God or a baby Beelzebub?

The answer depends on who you talk to. Let's take the dark side first. The 'original sin' argument suggests humans are born with depravity and corruption at our core.

It's a matter of taste, but personally I prefer the more forgiving Buddhist notion of the 'original face'. I can identify with Buddhism because if you see Polaroids of me when I was a baby, I had the 'original Buddha belly'. The original face means you arrived perfect. Pure. A blank slate waiting to be imprinted on. You were just a human being. Being you. Unadulterated. No added flavourings or colourings. There was no pretence, no shame, no trying to impress.

You had no idea about what football team you were gonna support – Wigan Athletic, Derby County – your authors must have been extraordinarily sinful in previous lives.

The baby version of you didn't know your Friday from your Monday. You didn't know school or work even existed. You experienced the world: squeezed it, licked it, sniffed it, stuck your fingers in it...

Exploring, curious, questioning. Your brain was a jello of connectivity. You – day 1 – were pure potential. You were also, by the way, full of love; 2 year olds, when they meet other 2 year olds, they hug, they share and they play.

All remains generally good and positive until your biological clock strikes teenage o'clock!

This is when the 'learned self' starts to creep in. There comes a point where your brain is sufficiently advanced to start thinking and reasoning for yourself. That's why teenagers kick back, push the boundaries and develop their own views and ideas about how the world works. Teenagers experience an overwhelming desire to fit in. Think back to when you were 14... you will have had the same haircut, worn the same clothes and listened to the same music as your besties.

Why? Because your tribe becomes all-important. Family can become very uncool so your dad, whom you worshipped last year, is now a huge embarrassment. In fact, your desire to fit into a peer group is so strong that it causes a whole lot of anguish if you're excluded.

Some research suggests the distress of not fitting in causes more discomfort than physical pain.

Crucially, you develop critical reasoning that allows you, for the first time, to see beneath the surface of situations and imagine hidden threats to your wellbeing. In simple English, that means you begin to imagine what others think about you. This realisation has huge connotations. Up until now you didn't care what anyone thought about you. It hadn't crossed your mind that anyone had an opinion of you. And all of a sudden, it dawns – you start having thoughts/opinions about other people (*oh my gosh what does she look like in those jeans?*) and BOOM, you realise other people are capable of having those exact same thoughts *about you*.

Yes folks, they're talking about you behind your back!

This is the birth of self-consciousness and the world gets very complicated very quickly. It becomes a game. You're going to need the right jeans, for a start. And to say the right things. And to fit into certain behavioural norms. That carefree version of you, the one that soaks up the world, the skipping, jumping in puddles, happy-go-lucky, daydreaming you, starts to hide.

Look around – right now. Hardly anyone is carefree and happy. Nobody skips to work. Often, it's the total opposite. Daydreams have turned into night sweats. Mondays – everyone's a bit glum. They're grumbling about the weather. The traffic is a nightmare. The news is negative. That's what people talk about and you learn to play the game. The 'fitting in' game. The original face wears a mask. You stop being you at your best and you start to be you at your fair-to-middling-est.

To be clear, nobody's born fair to middling. In the same way that nobody's born racist, or sexist, or evil, or ill mannered.

> **Nobody's born hating Mondays. Nobody's born complaining about the weather. Nobody's born with a dreary attitude.**

Nobody's born complaining about politics or the economy. Nobody's born with self-doubt.

These are all learned behaviours and *unlearning* can be a hard thing to do. Your brain isn't some perfectly sleek 5.0 model that's fully 21st-century compliant. The contents of your skull have evolved, slowly, with bits bolted on. Neurons that fire together wire together, so pathways have been grooved in. Software glitches have been patched, but not fixed. Your brain is riddled with malware. The human SPAM filter is fitted backwards so all the negativity pours in and the good stuff goes straight into your trash folder. As for those thought pop-ups... nothing seems to block them.

Basically, your wiring is haywire, but underneath it all

you've been hijacked by your basic operating system that treats danger like Velcro and happiness like Teflon.

Thus, it's easy to be locked down by a whoosh of very sticky negative emotions.

How can we prevent ourselves being hijacked by our emotions and being held hostage by them? One way to do so is to reflect on the following questions. Some will be more relevant than others, depending on your situation. As you read through them, keep an issue in mind that has caused you, or is causing you, some anxiety at the moment and see which questions are particularly helpful.

- Is the likelihood of this event occurring a nailed on certainty or just the vaguest of possibilities?
- If you had to place the event on a scale of 1–10, where 10 was the equivalent of the end of the world, where would it be?
- If your anxiety has been triggered by what you've read or heard, what is the source of the information? Is it reliable?
- Is what you're hearing from others 100% true – or is it opinion or speculation presented as fact?
- What ways can you influence or improve the situation? (If there aren't any, recognise there are occasions when you simply have to accept the reality of what you're facing. But remember, you might not always have control of the event, but you do have control over how you respond to it.)
- Are you giving yourself time to digest the facts and weigh up your options before making a decision or taking action?
- What's your relationship like with your anxiety – are you accepting it's OK to feel anxious without being over-whelmed by it, or have you become a hostage to it?
- Is there a person or a group of people you could talk to for their perspective who are less emotionally involved than you?
- How important will this issue be in 6 months' time?
- How effective has your current response been in dealing with the situation?
- What have you learnt from this experience that will help you going forward?
- Can you identify any positives to take from the situation?
- How would your best friend advise you to deal with the situation?

Perhaps it is time to live a better life by understanding what drives our instincts and impulses, and learning to acknowledge them but not be controlled by them. In which case some of the questions above might help you reflect and reframe. Perhaps they could be questions you also share with others who are struggling at the moment.

Personal change doesn't always come easily. We've developed a strong sense of who we are and what we're good and bad at.

> **Most functioning adults have an identity, part of which is shaped by a lifetime of accumulated emotional and psychological baggage.**

It's not as easy as just dropping your bad stuff in the baggage drop area and walking away.

If you want to change 'who you are' in the truest personal development sense of '*leaning into being your best self*' you need to rethink your thinking. Hope rests in neuroplasticity, the ability of the brain to shapeshift over time. The jello between your ears is an amazing piece of kit. Up until your teenage years you are a learning machine, with new pathways created and pruned. The pace of rewiring slows as you get older (which is why it's easy to get stuck in a rut of sameness) but

> **it remains perfectly possible for old dogs to learn new tricks.**

Crucially, the old dog has to have agency – that is, a belief that it is able to affect its outcomes. And secondly, the old dog needs to be willing to change. We're going to fall short of offending our readers by calling them 'old dogs' but the following questions remain pertinent.

To graduate to the next section, Dr Andy's science bit, you need to be able to answer positively to both...

Do you feel able to *influence your future*, and are you willing to give it *a damn good go?*

This next section introduces the basics, which sets us up for **THE HAPPINESS REVOLUTION** that follows. So furrow that brow, put your learning face on, and let's get those brain cells buzzing.

Here's some science...

FLIP IT

'The most difficult thing to learn is
something you think you know already.'
[Jiddu Krishnamurti]

Question for the over 50s: think back to your first few holidays, what
did you pack your clothes in?

Suitcases. Obviously.

And when you arrived at wherever you were going, what did you have to do?

Carry your suitcases. *Carry*. Not wheel.

Because your suitcases didn't have wheels.

The under 50s are reeling from this fact. Suitcases have been around for several hundreds of years. Wheels, even longer than that. But nobody had ever thought of putting the two inventions together. The most obvious combo, the bacon and eggs of travel, had gone un-thought-of.

I'm putting that out there as a prelude to something that, for me, falls into the same head-scratching category of 'why on earth did we not think of this earlier?'

The study of the human mind has been around since ancient civilisation began, but the starting pistol for modern psychology was fired in 1879 when Wilhelm Wundt sought to unpick it from philosophy, sociology and physiology. His Leipzig laboratory is widely acknowledged as the first of its kind.

For the next 100 years the field of psychology consisted of a rag-tag bunch of medical doctors, shrinks, geniuses, experimenters and charlatans, all doing their own thing. The early decades gave psychologists a ready-made cohort of 'lunatic asylum' patients who had no choice but to become subjects of experimentation. I haven't dared to dig too deeply because, quite frankly, I find it tremendously upsetting.

One of the most infamous chapters in the history of mental health 'treatments' was psychosurgery, a truly gruesome 'cure' where a doctor would hammer a medical instrument (similar to an ice-pick) through the top of both eye sockets. This would sever the nerves that connect the frontal lobes to the centres of the inner brain. The idea behind this surgery (better known as a lobotomy) was to induce calm in patients who were uncontrollably hysterical or emotional, especially in conditions like schizophrenia, manic depression and bipolar disorder.

To be fair, they were a lot calmer afterwards. Dead calm, mostly.

The case for the *defence* of psychology can be made succinctly. Most of the awful experiments date from back in the day, way before modern ethics had been invented.

Psychology is like the rest of us, it has plenty of skeletons in its cupboard.

Any glaring errors are obvious if viewed through the lens of today. Psychology's made huge strides in ethics and treatment. Millions of people have benefitted from counselling, therapy and medication.

All true. But the case for the prosecution is damning. I'm not so much talking about ethical skeletons. My argument is that, despite 150 years of research, no matter how much we spend or how much medical brain power we summon, psychological problems are getting worse not better.

The World Health Organization estimates that there are 800,000 suicides per year.[1]

Members of the jury, with that statistic alone, I put it to you that traditional branches of psychology are like King Canute. Although they mean well, they are not managing to stem the tide of mental ill health.

---

[1] https://www.who.int/news-room/fact-sheets/detail/suicide

Hence our revolution starts from the other end of the spectrum, a starting point so obvious and yet somehow hidden in plain sight. Put your hand up when you've spotted the pattern: child psychology looks at children who need help and behavioural psychology looks at ridding people of bad habits. Clinical psychology seeks to remedy mental disorders, cognitive psychology is applied to people who experience memory loss and learning disabilities. Counselling psychology is often associated with marriage and grief reparation. Developmental and educational psychology are most often about helping children catch up or manage their ADHD, dyslexia, etc. Forensic psychology gets into the minds of the criminally deranged.

Have you noticed?

Yes, these are worthy of study. All are useful and relevant. Groundbreaking remedies have stemmed from them. And yet, for the best part of 150 years, traditional strands of psychology have never studied people who are already happy.

All of a sudden it was a psychological case of *'Suitcase, meet the wheels. Wheels, meet the suitcase.'* We can all think of a handful of people in our lives who seem to take life in their stride. These people have energy, passion and a can-do mentality. They're not rich or famous. They're no cleverer than you or me. They don't have perfect lives but there's a certain 'something' about them. These happy few don't show up on social services' radar and their tendency to 'not be ill' deems them to be unworthy of the attention of the traditional psychological fraternity.

Cold-shouldered for too long, I decided to flip psychology on its head and give them a warm embrace. The handful you can think of right now – not only are they happy but they also have the power to light you up too! I sought to answer three simple questions:

1 **Who the heck are they?**

2 **What are the positive outliers doing that enable them to be/stay happier than the majority?**

3 **What can we learn from them – strategies that we can apply in our own lives so that we might elevate our levels of happiness too?**

As I admitted a few sentences ago, this is a bunch of obvious questions that have somehow been missed since psychology was invented.

This next page or two is a potted summary of my own research. Before the off, for the critics out there, I need to come clean on a couple of points. I have huge admiration for career academics who have the capacity to churn out paper after paper. During my research I got to know such people. I recently got an email from a university professor who had so many letters after her name that I thought she might have had a stroke and collapsed on her keyboard.

I am not that person. I'm more of a grafter.

My second admission is that I'm about to over-simplify 12 years of my academic life. The following diagram and the explanation that accompanies it – neither appear in my thesis. If you want 130k unexpurgated words, the PhD is downloadable from my website.[2]

Good luck.

Here it is for normal people.

---

[2] PhD thesis downloadable here: https://www.artofbrilliance.co.uk/resources/research/

I like to think of positive psychology as the study of what can go *right* with you. If you asked a whole bunch of people how happy they are and plotted them onto a happiness graph (which is what I actually did) it'd look a little bit like this...

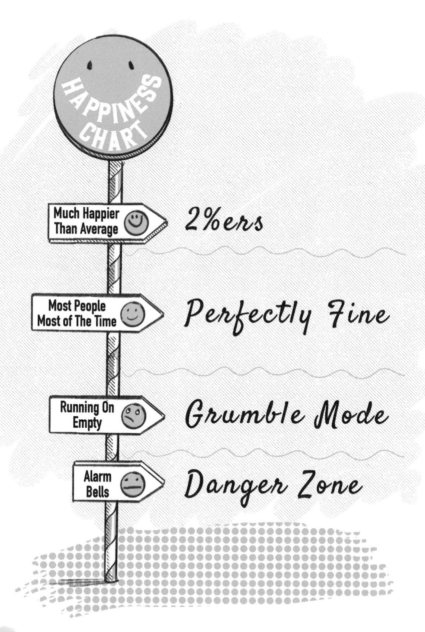

Much Happier Than Average — 2%ers

Most People Most of The Time — Perfectly Fine

Running On Empty — Grumble Mode

Alarm Bells — Danger Zone

I've presented this model to boardrooms and classrooms. It's not a difficult concept. For instance, I've never had an 8 year old raise their hand and say 'Gosh Dr Andy, this is terrifically complicated. I'm struggling to comprehend what it all means. Can you explain it again, but this time more simply?'

That conversation has never occurred. Why? Because even 8 year olds will intuitively grasp the simplicity what I'm talking about.

In the happiness chart, let's start in the 'perfectly fine' category. There's an adage in positive psychology that 'most people are mildly happy most of the time'. Obviously, there are huge exceptions but the adage holds true across the developed world. In the UK, for instance, our average happiness hovers around the 6.5 to 7.5 out of 10 mark.

So contrary to what we hear on the news, it's not all doom and gloom. Chin up. The happiness forecast is that most people are feeling fair-to-middling on Monday, improving to reasonably chipper after Wednesday with outbreaks of joy at weekends.

However, as we pointed out in Part 1, the world has upped its malevolence to the point where life's isobars conspire to bring some high pressure. Life can (and will) send occasional black clouds and squally showers. It's easy to slip into the grumble zone and, without really knowing it, you become trapped into a habit of low-level negativity. This saps your energy and you become expert at accidentally sucking all the positivity out of those around you, hence I sometimes call these people 'energy vampires'.

Please note, having spent the best part of four decades languishing in the grumble zone I can vouch for the fact that I am not knocking the afflicted. Those running on empty are perfectly nice people. There's nothing actually wrong with them other than that they've been battered by life and therefore gotten into a habit of being negative about pretty much everything. If I look back at the old version of me – the energy vampire – there was a lot of tutting, sighing, huffing, puffing and rolling of eyes. If I listened back to the me of old everything was 'unfair' or a 'nightmare'. Life was full of hassle, my soup was lukewarm, my job was boring, the weather was too hot (...cold, sweltering, rainy, foggy, cloudy, sunny, windy, snowy, misty, hurricaney, sleety – something-y). If you'd been cornered by me at a party you'd have been wishing you had a Netflix 'Skip Intro' button, but for conversations!

For the record, I wasn't ill. Just a bit stuck. My only 'affliction' is that I'd let life grind the passion out of me.

It's actually very easy to get trapped in the grumble zone and if you've been running on empty for too long, the wellbeing alarm bells start to ring. The bottom end of the happiness spectrum is the danger zone. This is where negativity can become pervasive and all-consuming. Too long in the danger zone means the warning siren becomes a deafening claxon. Happiness, hope and optimism can be drowned out and things can get serious.

This is where traditional psychology kicks in. Once you're diagnosed with a clinical disorder, the resolution profession will don their latex pants and superhero capes. Psychologists and medics will rally round. Counselling, CBT and/or meds will (should!) be available.

My point is that the psychological profession has spent 150 years investigating the danger zone while cold-shouldering those at the top end of the wellbeing graph.

So I reverse engineered the whole thing and came at psychology from the top end of the wellbeing spectrum. I studied the so-called 2%ers (named on the grounds that there aren't many around). Indeed, you can count your 2%ers on the fingers of one hand. A 2%er is someone whose upward levels of happiness and energy are of statistical significance. It's you with bags of energy, a beam etched across your chops and a spring in your step. It's my shorthand way of saying it's you at your best. You feel on top of the world, so if I bring you a problem when you're in 2% mode, it's less of a problem.

The difference between you at the top and bottom of the wellbeing graph is game changing. Life at the upper end of the happiness spectrum is everyday superhero status and the bottom end is you at your negative worst. Lousy. No energy. Zero enthusiasm. Straight mouth. The spring is replaced by a slouch.

If I bring you a problem there, it IS a problem. At the bottom end of the graph is everyday superZERO status.

Here are two fake illnesses, conjured by authors. I think they represent different ends of the 2%ers diagram:

'Gray Brittle Death' appears as a disease in the book 'The Color Out of Space'. See if you recognise the symptoms, either in yourself or someone you know: human victims describe 'being drained of something' or 'having the life sucked out'.

Contrast with Jim Davis' Garfield character, who contracted 'Hawaiian Cat Flu', a rare disease whose symptoms include a craving for Hawaiian pizza, a compulsion to wear loud shirts and an inability to resist hula dancing.

If you have accidentally slipped into the grumble zone, rest assured, it's perfectly possible to climb back onto the perch.

Indeed, the remainder of the book gives you a leg up to the top end of the wellbeing graph but there are a couple of very quick points before we move on.

Quick but BIG!

Firstly, being a 2%er will change your life for the better. It's probably the most important thing you will ever do. In fact, it doesn't just change your life, it impacts on those closest to you.

Second, you might have already worked that you already are a 2%er.

Sometimes!

We're interested in helping you get there more often.

And third, being a 2%er is a *learned* behaviour. Sure, you can have a bit of advantageous genetic jiggery pokery, but no matter where you are on the 2%ers diagram right now, you can learn a whole bunch of stuff that makes a difference.

THE EFF-WORD

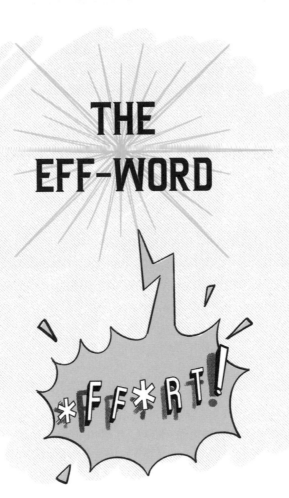

In true Columbo style... one last thing before we close Part 1 of
THE HAPPINESS REVOLUTION...

Think about it. Loads of adults go to the gym to work on their *physical*
strength. Some want to tone their bodies, develop some biceps, maybe
get a six-pack stomach. And to get physically fit, you don't just go to
the gym once and think, 'yep, that's me done'. You have to go regularly.
There's effort involved. And pain too, come to think of it. Oh, and if
you stop going, the bad bod soon comes back. Physical strength – if
there's one word that sums up how to get it – that word would be
'commitment'.

What most people don't realise is that it's also perfectly possible to develop *mental* strength – kind of like an emotional six-pack – a set of thinking skills that will allow you to cope with the weight of the world. Becoming a 2%er is like visiting a *mind* gym.

> **And to get emotionally and mentally fit, you don't just go to the mind gym once and think, 'yep, that's me done'. You have to go regularly.**

There's effort involved. And pain too, come to think of it. Oh, and if you stop going, the bad thinking habits soon come back. Mental strength – if there's one word that sums up how to get it – that word would be 'commitment'.

[Quizzical look] I've just had that déjà vu feeling.

Let's take the gym analogy a bit further. I've got a mate, Mick, who's been a paid-up member of his local gym for 4 years. Yes, the monthly fee has disappeared from his bank account every single month for 48 months. And yet he's never actually been to the gym. For the record, Mick's not especially rich. He's a normal bloke with a reliable wage but not a lot of spare cash. Yet he's willing to pay a monthly subscription to be a member of a gym he never goes to.

The interesting thing is, if you ask him why, he'll have a perfectly reasonable excuse: too busy, too tired, too rainy, 'not feeling it'. He once got as far as the car park but forgot his kit.

Here's the funny bit.

COVID-19 came along (sorry, that's not especially funny) and Mick's gym had to shut for 4 months (that's not funny either). Mick phoned his gym.

No answer. Furloughed. It transpires their policy is to do lots of online classes and to keep taking your monthly subscription even when the gym is closed.

This is a genuine conversation I had with Mick; 'I don't mind paying and not going,' he explained. 'So I'm happy to pay when I can go, but don't. But it really annoys me to pay when I can't actually go.'

I nodded. Furrowed brow. Pretending his logic made sense.

'So,' he nodded, 'I've cancelled my direct debit and I'll start paying again when it re-opens.'

'Gotcha,' I said, scratching my head. 'You don't mind paying and not going when it's open. But it upsets you to pay and not go when it's closed. So you'll pay and not go again as soon as it re-opens.'

'Exactly,' he said.

On a botheredness scale of 1–10, Mick's a 2.

Which brings us to the dreaded eff-word: effort!

Here is a plain and simple question that goes to the heart of your physical and mental fitness...

... Can you be bothered?

Let me ask it again with different emphasis.

Can *YOU* be bothered?

Because physical and mental fitness is about YOU being bothered about YOU. Your authors wanting physical and mental fitness for you is all well and good. But we can't be bothered *for* you.

And on that nonsensical note we endeth our Part 1 salvo. Yes, we've devoted a quarter of the book to 'context', making the case for why we need positive psychology in our lives. We've prepped you for what's about to come. The remainder of the book is solution focused.

Cast your mind back to the first chapter. We challenged you to make a new beginning. The truth? You cannot go back to the beginning and start again, but all of us can evaluate the heartbeats we have left and vow to make the best of what's to come. But a new beginning is absolutely NOT a new you. It's the 2% version of you. It's you before the world got its claws in. That smiley face, that energy, that love of life – they're the sexiest things ever, so why not wear them again?

It's not too late. It's never too late.

For Paul and me, it's never been about self-improvement. I mean, how could it be? You were born with so much to give. It's always been about self-*remembering*.

'Amazing' is who you really are.

You were born curious, questioning, with a thirst for learning. You were born to play. Pure potential. Pure love. If you're not currently feeling it, it's not lost, just forgotten.

So, may we finish this section by asking a favour? Find your botheredness and bring it to Part 2. When you show up, show up as that awesome version of you. The 2%er. It's what your family needs. It's what your work colleagues need. It's what you need. Scrub that. It's bigger.

You at your best, it's what the world needs.

We need **THAT** version to join the revolution. Remember the invite on page 9? The happiness revolution?

The invite still stands. It's time to unmute yourself in real life. Will the real you please step forward.

Part 2

MANIFESTO
[man-uh-fes-toh]

i A public declaration of intentions, objectives or motives.

ii A document that promotes a new idea with prescriptive notions for carrying out changes the author believes should be made.

All revolutions need a manifesto: a set of lofty aims that encourage people to sign up to the cause. Sadly, political manifestos have a bad name. They're often a long list of promises that get broken as soon as you've been conned into the ballot box.

Our HAPPINESS REVOLUTION manifesto pledges are different. They're not things *we're* promising to do, they're ideas that we'd like *you* to adopt, habits that are worth forming and promises we want you to keep. To *yourself*.

They are mostly common sense. Less so, common practice. Some pledges will jump out at you as immediately do-able, others might be more challenging. Our advice is to take them seriously, especially the weird and wonderful ones.

The following ten manifesto pledges are written like no other. Along the way you'll learn some new words and we're going to ask you to join a very long queue. There's a reminder about comedy great Dick Emery, and we talk about life's small print and Tourette's.

Part 2 is packed with fun. There are games galore: Snakes and Ladders, Hungry Hippos, Trivial Pursuit and our 'Grand Slam Values Challenge'.

You can also expect our Happiness Manifesto pledges to take you on a voyage to exotic places. Among the dreamy stop offs are India, Japan, Finland, Cameroon, Denmark, Turkey, Zimbabwe and – *ahem* – Ipswich.

Our crescendo is an invite to be an Olympic champion.

Deep breath. Onwards…

The Little Shop of Shame

Prescription: LOVE. Take as needed.

I'm lucky that as a keynote speaker I get to listen in on a lot of other keynote speakers. There's a circuit – entrepreneurs, leaders, gold medallists, authors, politicians, educators, OBEs, Sirs, Dames, celebs, comedians – and most are very very good. Often I'm pacing backstage, expectant father style, secretly hoping that the very very good won't be too good, because I've got to follow them!

After 20 years in the business you get to know the handful that are truly world class and, on this occasion, I was in for a treat. True to form, John delivered one of the most awesome talks I've ever experienced and, as is the way with world-class speakers, he made it seem effortless. With no visible sign of nerves, no notes and just a sprinkling of PowerPoints, his talk captivated an audience of nearly a thousand people. A keynote with belly laughs and tears is something to behold. His stories were well told, his humour hilarious, his insight insightful, his hard-hitting points landing like uppercuts.

John was as John always is: knockout.

Rather than be overawed, I decided to be just awed. I looked up to John and aspired to be like him. I loved the fact that he'd got the conference off to a flyer. I was nervous that the bar had been set at 'ridiculously high' but excited by the challenge of attempting to keep up with him. I wanted to connect with my audience not just intellectually but also emotionally, as John seemed to do so effortlessly.

He must have felt exhilarated as he took his seat alongside the host of the event. He had not quite received a standing ovation (this was a mainly British audience after all) but the applause was loud, enthusiastic and lingering.

Then, as he settled into his seat alongside the host, with his microphone still live, he could be heard to mutter these words, quietly but still audibly:

'Was I OK?'

Amazing eh?

This rock star with words, who had held the audience in the palm of his hand, still felt in need of reassurance. I wonder if three similar words form the underlying question that unconsciously drives all human behaviour:

'Am I OK?'

It brings us back to the ancients once again. Back in the day, a lone human on the savannah was a dead human. Separation from your tribe was a death sentence. To avoid death by rejection we developed an acute sense of what it takes to be accepted.

Perhaps that's why, from a survival perspective, our ancient brain still feels compelled to keep asking the same questions – 'Am I OK?', 'Did I do alright?', 'Do you still like me?' 'Have I got your approval?' –

because acceptance remains a fundamental human need. It's part of our survival software.

For some of us, no matter how often that question is answered affirmatively, we still feel the need for reassurance. We seek approval from many sources – from our loved ones, friends, colleagues, bosses and customers. But now with the impact of social media, particularly but not exclusively amongst the younger generation, our net is cast wider in our quest to gather the validation of total strangers – although we refer to these strangers as followers and friends.

THINKING *INSIDE* THE BOX:

Social media. It's taken me a while to realise that with Facebook, Insta, Twitter and the like, you and I are not the customer. The service is free. That means we're the *product*.

It takes a while for that nugget to settle. Basically, our attention is being sold. Your backstory, likes/dislikes/preferences, your friendship group, your clicks...these are being sold to marketeers. The FB, Insta, YouTube, TikTok, Twitter 'customers' (i.e., the ones who pay the money) are the advertisers. The data is mined. Algorithms are applied and a steady stream of suggestions comes your way.

Again, none of this is necessarily bad. It's how marketing has always worked. Just be aware. You are the product. More specifically, your *attention* is the product. Your attention has a price. If companies can snaffle your attention, you are more likely to buy their products/services.

Our accumulation of retweets, share, likes and followers has become an indicator of our value and status. Platforms that can facilitate connection have in turn fuelled comparison as we desperately want to know the answer to the question that nags deep inside us. Those three little words...

Am. I. OK?

Two things stand out.

Firstly,

> **we live in a world that actually benefits from us *not* feeling OK.**

A world that is skilled at magnifying our insecurities and cultivating our sense of unhappiness about who we are, what we do and – in an ever-increasingly image-conscious world – what we look like.

> **Our fundamental fears of not being good enough can be exploited by companies who profit from our sense of lack.**

They toy with our emotions by dangling the carrot of happiness and approval via a product or an experience. The pursuit of perfection is placed on a pedestal – a worthy and important goal that many of us buy into, in a desire to satisfy our insecurities and find acceptance.

Oh, and please don't think for one moment that I am immune to all of this. What we notice so clearly in others is often a reflection of our own struggles. I have not just sought acceptance – I've chased it relentlessly. For years, I bought wholeheartedly into the lie that I'm not OK and I made a huge emotional investment to remedy the fact.

And the consequences of doing so? Well, in my case I wouldn't allow myself to be happy until I reached a certain weight. My bathroom weighing scales became the arbitrator of my happiness. My joy lay in their hands.

I became obsessed. Early childhood experiences created a strong and deep connection between my appearance and my self-acceptance, and I discovered that humiliation is a strong driver for self-loathing.

Add into the mix that our primary instinct seems to have evolved from a need for food, shelter, and security to one of peer approval, is it any wonder that companies are so keen to create a sense of dissatisfaction or desire within us that can only be satisfied by a particular product – *theirs* – in order to satisfy the approval urge. And perhaps the question remains, despite the images we portray to others of how happy we are, am I, along with many others, simply papering over my feelings of inadequacy?

Are those feelings driven not just by a world that reminds me I need to be more, do more and spend more, but is there also a deeper and more powerful driver that creates the desire to answer the question, 'Am I OK?'

Is that 'something' actually ourselves?

The reality is that deep down, no one knows us better than us… right? If I was on *Mastermind*, my chosen expert subject would be 'me', and yours 'you'. We're the world experts.

Objectively, if I stand back and reflect on my life, it's nothing short of amazing. I have a wonderful family. I love my job and when I pass through an airport or station, there are books in the shops with my name on the cover. At a logical level you'd think I'd be heel-clicking through my days, and yet I'm honest enough to admit I have a PhD in insecurity and I'm a world expert in 'imposter syndrome'. It's fair to say that a lot of my everyday thoughts wouldn't go in my *'stuff I'm really proud of'* box.

Let's put it this way: if there was a box marked *'shame'*, I might negoti-ate a discount due to the number of boxes I'd need to purchase. What's more, I suspect that when I show up to collect my boxes from the Little Shop of Shame, there would be a queue that stretches down the street and around the corner. We'd shuffle along patiently, making small talk with our fellow shame queuers, and we'd find that we're all needing 'shame boxes' for the same kinds of things: guilt, embarrassment, inadequacy, stuff you did way back, the way you treated someone at school, a bout of bad parenting, belittling someone in a meeting, body image, your dad passing away before you'd had time to make peace with him, the time you cheated in an exam, the time you cheated on your spouse, your failure to live up to your potential, the character assassination tweets you sent...

The Little Shop of Shame is a little shop of horrors.

Bottom line – some people struggle to be their own best mate because, perhaps at a subconscious level, they're thinking 'if you knew the real me you wouldn't love and accept me either'.

> **Here's the deal – the fact is that to a greater or larger extent we are all a mixture of flaws and failings, mixed in with our 'fantastics'.**

I think we need to think about ourselves and other people in less black and white terms. We're not good or bad.

We're a combination of both.

Admittedly, some people swing the other way. Self-love, self-care and self-acceptance should never develop into a full-blown love affair with yourself. I'm reminded of these words from my great friend Dave Hill: 'Too much selfie isn't healthy.'

Academic studies point to narcissism being on the rise.[1] While it might seem appealing to be able to swashbuckle through life, your chest puffed full of your own self-importance, oblivious to your flaws and failings, I'm advocating a much quieter love affair.

There are plenty of things that fall into the category of best thing since sliced bread. I'd go as far to say that you are even better than whatever came *before* anyone even thought of the concept of sliced bread. And I'm not even joking.

You are bloody amazing.

The narcissists will proclaim it to the world, whereas I'm advocating that you start closer to home.

YOU ARE BLOODY AMAZING! Announce it to yourself.

It's a great place to start the repairing process. It's the ring on the finger of a beautiful relationship: you in holy matrimony with you. Flaws and all. Go down on one knee and ask yourself if you'd like to spend the rest of your life with yourself. Begin a lifetime love affair. Passionate, happy, sharing in the highs and lows.

You with you. Dust to dust, for richer or poorer, may the force be with you, because you're worth it. Amen and all that.

To consummate the relationship, here are a couple of points to ponder.

---

[1] Why Is Narcissism Increasing Among Young Americans? https://www.psychologytoday.com/gb/blog/freedom-learn/201401/why-is-narcissism-increasing-among-young-americans

Kiss the Frog, Warts and All

Most self-help books will tell you what I've just told you: you are amazing. But the truth is that you won't feel amazing all the time.

And that's OK.

You'll have your shitty days that will often be accompanied by shitty thoughts and behaviours. You're still amazing, though. Just not perfect.

The Japanese have a word for it: *wabi-sabi*. This wonderful concept is founded on three simple realities: nothing lasts, nothing is finished, and nothing is perfect. *Wabi-sabi* hasn't got a direct English translation but it encapsulates the essence of being perfectly imperfect. It's often applied to art and pottery. So, for example, drinking your hot chocolate from your favourite rustic mug is *wabi-sabi*. Not only are you comfortable with the fact that the mug is simple, rustic and chipped, but its lack of class somehow adds to your drinking pleasure.

The Japanese don't generally apply the principle to people, but they're missing a trick. *Wabi-sabi* maps across effortlessly. Remember, *nothing lasts, nothing is finished,* and *nothing is perfect.* Including all 7.5 billion of us. That means your quirks, anomalies and imperfections are the most beautiful things in the world. Your lack of class is somehow classy! That mole on your chin, that slightly crooked nose, your wonky feet, those few straggly strands of hair that refuse to behave, those wrinkles around your eyes, your shyness, your muffin tops, your cellulite, the way you blush, the fact you can't take a compliment, your gappy teeth, you could do with being a couple of inches taller – or shorter – the sleep in your eye, your scruffy jeans, your insecurities, your saggy bits, your fear of spiders, your terrible parking, your snoring, your coffee breath, the fact that you'd prefer to stay in than go to the party, the fact you're still smarting from a comment a teacher made 30 years ago…

…Your foibles. Your uniqueness.

I am most definitely *wabi-sabi*. You are *wabi-sabi*. *Everyone* is *wabi-sabi*. We're all human beings, beautifully crafted by wear and tear.

You are flawed beauty.

Revel in your imperfections. They make you, *you*.

Being happier means learning to live with, accepting and smiling at your flaws and failings.

Oh, and it helps if you understand that nobody else really cares about your *wabi-sabi*. Often, they haven't even noticed your imperfections because they've been so busy worrying about their own.

Speak to Yourself Like You Would a Friend

Tourette's Syndrome gives us a clue. This cruel affliction is rendered doubly mean because the sufferers always seem to be such lovely people. And yet here they are, the world's most fabulous humans blurting out the most obscene statements.

Tourette's sufferers rarely blurt out compliments or wonderfully warm words – 'Gosh, you're amazing' or 'Wow, I'm so lucky' – because that's not what's going through their minds.

Their control mechanism has gone haywire. Tourette's shows what a fine line it is. *Your* thought processes are equally vitriolic. All Tourette's sufferers are doing is shouting out what everyone else is actually thinking. The difference is that most of us are able to moderate the internal diatribe and keep our real thoughts to ourselves.

You are a snap-judgement machine.

> **The inner critic is always there. You can't turn it off, but you can turn it down.**

The late British entertainer Dick Emery, who was at the height of his fame in the 1970s, had a catchphrase: 'You are awful, but I like you.' To some extent I need to say to myself 'Paul, at times you are awful and you're capable of awful things – but I like you.' I confess it's not as catchy or succinct as Dick Emery's, but hopefully you get my point.

> **We're a cocktail of paradoxes and none of them are called 'perfection'.**

Think of how you are with a friend when they're going through a rough time. Think about the words you say and the tone in which you say them. I doubt the phrase 'you're such a loser' is uttered much, or even at all. Neither will you be telling them to give up on life and passively accept their fate.

If you have a friend in need, you'll be kind and encouraging, for sure. If you're a real mate you will even, when appropriate, challenge your friend. You won't necessarily subscribe to 'tough love' but you will 'love tough'. If your friend has done something stupid you'll be keen to understand why, but slow to offer excuses for their behaviour. You'll challenge appropriately and help them find ways forward. You won't help them search for a get-out-of-jail card – but neither will you con-demn them outright.

**Top tip:
You don't have to
attend every
argument you're
invited to.**

So how about you treat yourself in the same way?

Love tough.

How?

Challenge yourself from a place of compassion, not condemnation. The inner critic needs to become a critical friend. Recognise the para-dox of being you, but refuse to use it as an excuse. Give yourself another chance. Go again.

Focus on taking small steps. Remind yourself of how far you've come. Reach out for support. Celebrate successes, whilst still accepting you've still a way to go. As my late friend Joy Marsden would say, 'Keep stepping.'

Through my own struggles and life experience I've come to this realisa-tion. You can never experience real happiness when you have feelings

of shame as your constant companion. Learn to accept yourself –
which is different from approving of everything you've done. It's not
easy, but remember the long queue at The Little Shop of Shame? It's a
loooooong one.

Your authors are in it too. Shuffling forward. If you see us, give
us a wave.

Unplugged

2020 Lockdown gave me the opportunity to audit my life. I got a B+.
'Working hard but lacks focus. Could do better.'

Here's my report, and remedy.

The modern world has encroached, sort of wheedled its way into my
life in all sorts of sneaky ways. For a starter, all this Googling is making
me stupid. I'm checking emails while the kettle boils. I'm WhatsApping
my mates instead of phoning them. Comedy cats have hijacked my
attention. I'm scrolling instead of strolling. My satnav has caused me
to lose any sense of direction. Social media has made me anti-social.
Business-wise, I'm all Zoomed out. Binge-watching has robbed me of
my love of reading. My smartphone is waking me in the dead of night.
My heated driver's seat is making me soft. Just Eat is making me fat.
Deliveroo is making me lazy. I'm connected to wi-fi but less to my
family. It's a paradox, but every moment I capture on my camera is a
moment missed.

We've all got important decisions to make. I can play my King Canute
card and drown as the tech tide rages in, or I can take action. The
question for me was where to start? It turned out that the answer was it
doesn't matter where you start, what matters is that you do.

Last year I started messing around with what I called 'tech-NO-Friday'. It was an experiment. With the tide of modernity sweeping in, tech-NO-Friday was a test to see if I could keep it at bay for a seventh of my life.

Please note, I'm not being stupid about it. I'm no luddite. I've not gone 'tech vegan', just 'tech veggie'. Wi-fi lite. Friday means zero checking of emails, social media lockdown, no scrolling through the endless loop of web pages and my smartphone is turned off. I know. It'll send a shiver down your spine, like it did mine. But keep an open mind on 24 rock-solid hours of tech lockdown.

Let me tell you what happens. Your wi-fi connection is replaced by a different kind of connection: walking, mountain biking, reading (a book, not my Kindle), chatting, laughing, sitting, strolling (not scrolling), relaxing, eye contact and eating soup.

Yes, I often work Fridays but my tech-lite rule means I'm minimalist. I might have to tap away at my laptop (it'll be in flight mode). I might even have to plug it into a projector. But all the other tech-no rules apply, including no Friday satnav and no heated seat.

I can report that Friday quickly became bliss. It actually feels a little bit naughty. It's like a long weekend. Every weekend. I'm reconnected with my family, re-connected with me and therefore plugged back into life.

So that's it from now on. It's only 14% of my life but if I can reclaim that, I've already discovered that I'm refreshed, rejuvenated and better able to deal with the other 86.

Dr A x

Solemnly Swear to be Your Own Bestie

Manifesto reminder

1 It's comforting to know that the world's most amazing people also struggle with the same issues as us mortals! We all have 'acceptance issues'.

2 The truthful answer to the questions 'Am I okay?' and 'Am I enough?' are 'Hell yeah!' and 'You're way more than enough. You're nothing short of amazing!'

3 Despite us telling you the truth in point 2, you will still be dogged by insecure thoughts and nagging doubt. Companies know this. They want to sell you things so they prey on these insecurities: *buy our thing to fill your gap.*

4 The truth – again – is this: If there's something missing in your life it's probably you.

5 It's time to start a lifetime love affair: *you* with *you.*

6 You are beautiful *because* of your imperfections.

7 Commit to turn your inner critic into a critical friend.

8 Experiment with less tech. Invest that extra time with real flesh and blood people.

The 'I's Have It. But Which I, Ipswich or India?

It was a misty day and a young boy and his father were out fishing in the middle of a lake. The boy, perhaps caught up in the silence and the solitude of the experience, or maybe just bored, started to do what kids do. Peering into the near distance he inquired of his father, 'Daddy, why is the mist grey?'

Eyes fixed on the float, his father replied, 'I don't know, son.'

A few minutes later, dipping his hand in the lake, the lad asked, 'Daddy, why is water wet?'

The rowing boat wobbled a little as his father shifted uncomfortably in his seat. 'I really don't know, son.'

Moments later the silence was broken again. 'Daddy, how does this boat float on the water?'

The little boy waited while his father took a big breath, presumably seeking a deep answer. After a long exhale came his wisdom, 'I don't know, son.'

More questions followed: how do fish breathe underwater, how long do worms live, how many trees do you think there are, do you think a fly could ever cause an aeroplane to crash… with his father pausing to think before offering the exact same answer; 'I don't know, son.'

'Do you mind me asking you all these questions, dad?'

To which his father replied, 'Not at all, son. If you don't ask questions you'll never learn anything.'

The story made me smile but it also brings me onto a **BIG** question. **THE** question. The **WHY** question.

Why do you get out of bed in the morning?

Or even bigger, *why do you exist?*

My guess is that a life without meaning and purpose would have a big hole in it. A **YOU**-shaped hole. Here's the bottom line. Ultimately, we all need a sense of meaning and purpose to our lives, whether we're aware of it or not. But just like the father in the boat with his son, when asked the question 'what is the meaning and purpose to your life' our answer might echo a familiar response:

'I don't know, son.'

So why is 'why?' such a big deal and why could a lack of purpose and meaning be detrimental to our happiness? My own happiness data pointed to something really rather strange. On a scale of 1–10, where 1 is Eeyore and 10 is Tigger, we're fluctuating between 7.2 and 7.5.[1] Most people rate themselves as mildly happy in the here and now.

That's not the strange bit. The weird fact is that almost everyone predicts they will be happier in the future than they are right now.[2] Of course, if you're not in a very good place right now, it makes perfect sense to imagine that you'll dig yourself out of the mire and be in a better place 5 years hence.

But happy people also view a bright light at the end of the tunnel, even though their tunnel is already superbly lit. And exactly the same rule also applies to really *really* happy people. They're gonna need shades because in 5 years' time it's going to be dazzling. It struck me as curious. Whatever your happiness score right now – whether you're a 1, 6 or 9.6 out of 10 – you're predicting a happier you in 5 years' time. Even more bizarrely, those who currently rated their happiness as 10 out of 10 were also predicting a happier future. With the 10 out of 10s predicting they'll be 11, I had to investigate.

....
[1] The World Happiness report gives figures for most countries. The 7.5 out of 10 figure quoted was for the UK which compares to most of the western world. For Sub-Saharan Africa and war torn countries the stats are grim: https://worldhappiness.report/
[2] A stat from Andy's research, downloadable here: https://www.artofbrilliance.co.uk/resources/research/

It turns out that this pattern of expecting the future to be brighter than today is not a quirk, it's very much part of the human way. Of course, academics have a name for it: 'positive illusions'. It's a bit like being stuck in an existential weather forecast of 'overcast today' but 'gloriously sunny tomorrow'. Although these mental biases are incorrect (sadly, your happy tomorrow is like the real tomorrow – it never actually arrives), they serve an important evolutionary purpose.

Optimism serves as a biological necessity. Basically, we believe that the next 10 years will be better than this because otherwise we'd give up on our rather mundane existence. The point is better understood if you work logic the opposite way. Imagine for a moment if our prehistoric ancestors from around 200,000 years ago – let's call them Bob and Belinda – had mental software that predicted an okay today and less happy tomorrow. Now imagine that was repeated every single day.

Their stone-age optimism would be killed stone dead. The chances are Bob and Belinda's descendants (us!) would still be in our caves, scared stiff of our less happy future. Hence, our software program runs in the opposite way. Installed at the heart of being human is a desire to survive, to pass on our genes and overcome challenges in pursuit of that red sky at night, that sheer delight, over there on the horizon. So off we trudge. We have an inner longing to achieve, to make progress in order to improve our lives.

In a nutshell, we're wired for purpose – not for chilling in bed all day binging Netflix and eating Doritos. Purpose drives forward momentum. Whether we ever arrive at our predicted future happiness utopia is a moot point – the fact is that our *positive illusion* is enough to drive us forward, sniffing a wonderful carroty horizon.

Now no self-respecting book that looks at the subject of purpose and meaning would be complete without referring to the work of Viktor Frankl. If the name isn't familiar, he wrote the iconic book *Man's Search for Meaning* in which he describes his experiences in Nazi concentration camps during World War II. As you can imagine, it's not big on laughs, but it's HUGE on learning. Frankl observed that the prisoners most likely to survive the horrors of their experience were those who retained a sense of purpose – that their lives still mattered, and that they couldn't give up because they still had things they wanted to do with their lives. Frankl's words are hard going. He speaks of grown men just giving up. Physically they had enough strength to survive, but with all hope extinguished their bodies just gave up. Frankl himself, although much weaker than most, survived Auschwitz, fuelled by his carroty horizon that he called 'hope'.

However, the problem with having a sense of purpose is an idea that's been hijacked by some parts of the self-help brigade. It's often portrayed as a near-mystical concept – a puzzle that needs to be unlocked – if only you could find the key. And for some bizarre reason this key is often to be found in one particular place.

India!

Indeed, only last year my esteemed co-author jacked it all in and went on a 3-month walkabout, just him and a backpack, to 'find himself'. Guess where? Yep, some remote Himalayan village in northern India [face palm!]

He didn't go to, say, Ipswich. He didn't phone me up and say 'Prof, I need to go in search of the meaning of life so I've booked some time off to stay in a Premier Inn in a mid-sized town in Suffolk beautifully situated on the banks of the river Orwell. And guess what, I've treated myself to a family room.' With the whole world to choose from, he didn't go to Belgium or Uruguay. Or Rotherham. Or Fleetwood. Nope. He chose 3 months sitting cross-legged in a remote holy place by the Ganges.

So that gives us an opportunity to demystify the whole idea of meaning and purpose by playing a game of compare and contrast. One of us has done the '3-month retreat to a remote village in India' while the other one played the 'staying at home in Warrington' card.

So who learned the most?

We both agree that finding your purpose doesn't have to involve some dramatic experience. You don't need to attend an exclusive retreat in the mountains. No encounters with gurus are required. No truths need unlocking and no secrets need revealing.

But we'd like that, wouldn't we? We would like the romance and intrigue of it all. Dr Andy's got some great stories to tell his mates in the pub while, to be fair, my 3 months in Warrington got a bit samey. Taking on board the down-to-earth, no-bull advice from some short bloke currently based in Warrington is far less sexy.

And I get that. For the record, yes, Andy came home with some cool stories and life experiences, but also dysentery.

After comparing and contrasting, we both agree that life is about finding the special in the so-called ordinary. It's about learning to appreciate and recognise the incredible privilege we all have to be experiencing life on this planet right now. Moreover, it's about realising that the questions to ask are not 'What is the meaning of life?' but rather 'How can I give meaning to life?' That, although it's good to wrestle with the question 'Why are we here?' it's even better to ask, 'What can I do with my time here?'

That's when the rubber really hits the road.

Our point is this. In answer to the question – what's *your* purpose? – we've no idea. But if both or either of your parents are alive, then maybe part of your purpose is to be a half-decent son or daughter. If you've got kids then part of your purpose might be to instil in them a sense of knowing that they're loved, and to try and avoid passing on to them some of the screwed-up, twisted ideas about life that you've acquired so far, and instead pass on as much of the good stuff as possible.

Maybe part of your purpose is simply *not* to take life for granted. To quote the Jewish philosopher and theologian Abraham Heschel:

> 'Our goal should be to live life in radical amazement...
> Get up in the morning and look at the world in a way that
> takes nothing for granted. Everything is phenomenal,
> everything is incredible, never treat life casually.'

Sound advice eh?

Now I know we're all on our own unique journeys. I recognise that some people are driven by incredibly lofty goals. And that's to be applauded. I have friends that gave up their comfortable middle-class lifestyle in Warrington to work with some of Europe's poorest people in Macedonia. Some people's sense of purpose drives them to make incredible sacrifices or to spend their lives fighting for a particular cause. Brilliant. The by-product of all this will be a sense of fulfilment and an underlying sense of happiness.

But can I give a shout out to the billions of people who've come to realise that you don't have to do something earth-shattering to have lived a purposeful existence. What's the point of having a belly if there's no fire in it? Remembering that our pledge is called 'vow to relight your fire', perhaps rather than 'find your fire' you simply need to find a match. In fact, how about you make lots of fires.

> **You don't have to limit yourself to finding your one big purpose – how about embracing lots of them.**

They'll change throughout your life – a young, free, single, no-commitments person will prioritise a different purpose than when they're older. My mum's sense of purpose when she was young was to own her own house by the time she was 21. It fuelled her fire. Now her sense of purpose as a woman touching 80 is to be a generous grandma to my kids and still warn me to drive carefully when the roads are icy.

My friend Dorothy has dementia. When my wife and I visit she's always pleased to see us, although she has no clue who we are. But she still has a sense of purpose. She knits baby outfits for a charity that works in Africa. She sings in a choir. Is she happy? You bet. Is my mum happy? Absolutely.

Have either of them been on a retreat to India? Not that I'm aware of – although Dorothy was born in Ipswich.

So let's stop complicating the idea of finding your purpose. If you believe your life is pointless, that is a recipe for unhappiness – so having a sense of purpose is crucial to your wellbeing.

Your calling isn't to be found in some far-off distant land and it doesn't have to be on the horizon. It might not be revealed via a great bright light. There will almost certainly be no trumpet fanfare or a big neon arrow declaring '**PURPOSE**: next left turn'. Your purpose might not be discovered on the top of a mountain and, truth be told, you're just as likely to find it in Ipswich as you are India because it's most often to be found right under your nose. So do what floats your boat. Follow your curiosity. Take note of what makes you angry. Develop your strengths. Pursue your passions. If you're looking for a sign to show you your purpose, these are them.

These simple signs are all valid indicators. Clues. And if you try something and go along a particular path and find it's not for you, fine. Relax. The universe just gave you some feedback. You're not a tree. You don't have to stay where you are. Try another track. Pursue another route. Remember you're not lost – you're just exploring.

So start by stoking your internal boiler. Let your fires be the catalyst for others to start making their own.

And save your air fare to India.

Activity

Imagine you're 109 years old and, may I say, in very fine fettle. Must be all that oily fish?

Imagine you're looking back on your life as it is it TODAY. Then finish the following sentences:

I spent too much time worrying about…

I spent too little time doing things such as…

If I could go back in time, then what I would do differently from today onward is…

Vow to Relight Your Fire

Manifesto reminder

1. There's a lot of hoo-ha written about purpose and meaning. The truth is that everyone has a purpose. If you sit night after night watching TV and eating Doritos you are living out your purpose. Admittedly, it might not be a particularly dynamic or energising one, but it is a purpose.

2. Upgrading your purpose and then living *on* purpose – gosh! You'll feel energised. Things will start to happen.

3. Lots of people go to far-flung places to find themselves. India's popular. Ipswich less so. You'll find your best self much closer to home!

MANIFESTO PLEDGE #3

MAKE AN OATH TO YOUR PHYSICAL SELF

Top tip:
That body of yours, it's given to you
as a gift. There's no receipt. You can't
return or exchange it, so make the best
of it. Don't abuse it. Don't exhaust it.
Don't leave it lying around in the
sun for too long.

THE YEAR I CAUGHT UP WITH ME

1989 was an interesting year for me. When I say 'interesting' I mean it was bloody awful.

I became ill with myalgic encephalomyelitis, better known as ME or chronic fatigue syndrome. *Newsweek* wrote an article referring to it as the 'yuppie flu', which compounded my suffering. Not only had I contracted the world's most dubious illness, something the article described as 'a fashionable form of hypochondria', but I lost my job as a result.

My ME seemed unshakeable. The fatigue worsens with physical or mental activity, but doesn't improve with rest. It was the start of an incredibly challenging few years, where a walking stick became my best friend and I sometimes lacked the energy to even wash myself.

1989 was also a significant year for a bloke called Stephen, a somewhat older individual than me, based in Utah in the USA. His surname was Covey and his new book *The Seven Habits of Highly Effective People* was destined to sell over 30 million copies.

Nineteen years after *Seven Habits* was published and Covey was seen as the world's leading authority on leadership, we got to work together. Seriously, no joke, we did. The wee man from Warrington got to share a stage with the big bloke from Utah. We were both speakers at a real estate conference at the Sydney Convention Centre. Covey was the opening speaker on day two of the conference, and I followed him on the programme. Andy, who always likes to encourage me, would frame that as 'Stephen Covey was your warm-up act, mate.'

I didn't quite see it like that. I was simply in awe at the thought of meeting this A-lister of the personal development world. I remember our encounter vividly. We both arrived early in the morning to do a sound check. I'm not sure if he wanted a chat, but I was determined he was going to get one. I was keen to talk to him about leadership and it turns out that all he wanted to talk about was his grandchildren.

Seriously.

He had 52. I was tempted to ask if he could remember all their names – but the conference was due to start in two hours, and I hadn't had breakfast.

So I asked him about his habits instead. The ones in his book, I mean. His book listed seven and I was keen to know if there was one habit more important than any other. 'They're all important, Paul, but you've got to start with the first.'

I nodded as if I knew instantly what the first habit in the book was.

I didn't.

Sensing the awkwardness of the silence, being the big man that he literally was, Covey dug me out of my hole. Now clearly I wasn't secretly recording him, but here's the gist of what he said. '*Be proactive* is where you have to start. Focus on your circle of control and influence. Too many people focus on what concerns them but they can't do anything about.'

Although Stephen Covey is no longer with us, fortunately his messages live on.

Let's be honest, there's a lot going on in life where we have no control or real influence. Covey's point is that we can become fixated on what worries us but we can't do anything about. And the more you focus on the stuff you can't control, the less time you have to explore the areas you can.

Now this next point is crucial – so much so, it's in italics.

In a climate where there's so much in our outer world we're unable to influence, it's important to remember there's a lot in our inner world that we can.

If there's anything the global pandemic taught us – and I think there were some very loud and clear messages – it's don't take your health for granted. And that, my friend, is something that is largely in your control. The bottom line – it's hard to be happy when you're feeling physically lousy. And yes, I'm aware that previous sentence is right up there in the running for the 'Stating the Bleeding Obvious' award. But I wonder if we've passively accepted that our health is simply down to our genes, our upbringings, our environment, etc. – and that it's the responsibility of health professionals to make us well when we're sick.

I'd like to suggest that one way we could support our beloved NHS is to become less reliant on it. Changing a poor diet and taking more exercise may ultimately be an even greater expression of appreciation to our health service than clapping on your doorstep.

The previous paragraph comes with caveats. I appreciate people are born with health conditions and that fate isn't always kind in relation to our genetic make-up. Indeed, I fully accept my 3-year skirmish with **ME** is a reminder that sometimes ill health just happens.

But I'll go back to my dear friend Mr Covey (hey, we must have spoken for nearly 8 minutes, so I reckon that constitutes a deep and close friendship). We have to accept there are things out of our control – which includes stuff from our past – but what ultimately improves our life satisfaction is focusing on what we can do something about that is within our control.

So if you want to take better care of yourself – and I realise you may be doing a good job already – let me recommend the following.

A Nod to the Future You

Thought: 'Fast food'. Should it be a silent 's'?

I once told an audience that you are what you eat and a lady replied, 'I must be made of cake then!'

Well, the truth is that she's actually made of exactly the same thing as you and I. Cells. Atoms. Pure energy, actually. You are made of 37 trillion cells that have somehow combined to form you. And those 37 trillion cells have somehow learned to walk and talk and text and poo.

But here's the thing. Each of your cells is programmed to die. In fact your cells are quite heroic, they *have* to die, so you can live. Through a process of apoptosis each cell carefully destroys itself. Every single cell contains a poison gene called P53 which, once self-administered, causes the cell to shrink, destroy its basic proteins, dismantle its own DNA, thus allowing itself to be swallowed up by white blood cells and taken away. The cell self-sacrifices, being super careful to leave no trace. And, by the way, it does all this when it's in a healthy state.

Some cells only live a few hours. Taste buds, for example, only have a day or two, then they die and new ones pop up. Liver cells, they regenerate every 14 weeks or so. Colon cells, they live the longest.

The point being, every cell in your body dies and is replaced. The whole process takes about 6 months. So, thinking about it, 6 months from now, you will be an entirely new you! Literally, a completely different 37 trillion cells.

The big question is therefore, what kind of YOU do you want to be? An XXXXL you made of sugar, or a wholesome you, made of something more substantial?

Kummerspeck [German]: Excess weight gained from emotional overeating. Literally, 'grief bacon'.

Hara Hachi Boo is a wonderful Japanese concept that literally translates as 'stop eating just before you're full'. If you bear in mind that your stomach is about as big as your fist – *one* fist – that amount of food will suffice. It requires a whole load of rewriting of cultural habits that you probably grew up with. I, for example, was always encouraged to eat everything on my plate otherwise I'd get no pudding. It turns out that our family policy of 'eat until it hurts' might not be so good for a long and healthy life.

So eat slowly. Savour each mouthful. And stop eating just before you're full. Contrary to what your Neolithic brain will be screaming, you *do* actually know when you're next meal's coming. I promise you it'll be along in about 4 hours.

Activity

List all the substances and strategies you have ever used to try and feel better, including foods, drinks, cigarettes, recreational drugs, prescription drugs, exercise, sex, jaffa cakes, etc.

Once you've done that, go through your list and for each item, ask yourself:

1 Did this get rid of my painful thoughts and feelings in the long term?

2 Did it bring me closer to a rich, full and meaningful life?

3 If the answer to question 2 is 'no', then what did this cost me in terms of time, energy, money, health, relationships and vitality?

There's a lot written about self-care. Most of which makes perfect sense. But some things remain hidden in plain sight. They're so obvious and yet so easy to miss. Here's a simple self-care principle that eluded me until very recently.

Eat, move and sleep are keystone habits. If you get those right, everything else seems an awful lot easier. The missing link in all three is to be kind to yourself now, whilst keeping an eye on the wellbeing of your *future* self.

It's a game changer.

For example, after a particularly gruelling day in which everything that could go wrong did go wrong, you slump through the door and treat yourself to a glass of wine. You deserve it. It's self-care. In fact you're so caring that you have another, then a third, at which point you might as well finish the bottle.

That might make the present version of you feel relaxed and happy but at the expense of tomorrow's you. So self-care – with an eye on the wellbeing of the future you – means you stop at one glass. Or you have a cup of tea instead. That's caring for your 37 trillion cells now whilst also being kind to tomorrow's you who can rock up at work with renewed energy and vigour rather than lethargy and a hangover.

Food? Same. Devouring an entire packet of biscuits might feel like self-care right now. But the future you will suffer. So one biscuit and the packet goes away.

Exercise? Same. Skipping your bike ride might feel great in *this* moment. Indeed, it might feel genuinely caring to sit and binge-watch your fave Netflix series. Repeated night after night after night… your future self will be struggling for vitality.

Being kind to tomorrow's, next week's, next month's, next year's you…
it's a small change that makes a BIG difference.

Make it a Million

**Thought:
Sitting is the new smoking. Sleep
deprivation is the new saturated
fat. Six Red Bulls is NOT the
answer. Regular exercise and
good sleep hygiene – they
are the answers.**

A human being contains about eight pints of the good stuff. Blood flow
flushes away toxins as well as transporting nutrients, including oxygen,
to every cell in your body. Your brain makes up only 2% of your body's
weight, yet it uses 20% of the oxygen and blood flow in your body.
Therefore, anything that damages your blood vessels or impairs blood
flow hurts your brain. This means that taking care of your heart and
blood vessels to ensure healthy blood flow to your brain is not just important for your physical health, but it is also essential for your mental
wellbeing. If you want to keep your brain healthy, your mind sharp, and
your mental health strong for as long as possible, you need to protect
your blood vessels.

That means happiness and exercise are good bedfellows.

When someone mentions the word 'exercise' how does that make you feel? What images does it conjure up? Playing football with your mates? Dancing with friends? Hot sweaty gyms? Whatever the images and feelings it conjures up, the reality is a lack of exercise could be undermining your happiness.

But here's the curious thing. Initially, *not* exercising might actually make you feel happier. You see, there's an immediate payoff to taking the easy comfortable option. And that's what staying indoors, cosying up on the couch and binge-watching Netflix can provide.

Exercise takes effort, and often that means we need to override our body's natural disposition to save energy.

On a personal level, it took me ages to figure out that exercise energised me. How can burning all those calories on a 2-hour mountain bike ride make me feel amazing? Surely I should come home and collapse in a heap?

But those in the know, know. Gym, football, Zumba…whatever…there's an afterglow. Afterwards, you're buzzing. Although it's sometimes called 'runner's high', it's common across all forms of aerobic exercise.

But what if that's not you? What if the seduction of comfort seems too enticing? What if even the very thought of exercise triggers a mild allergic reaction?

Well I've got good news. Seriously, I have.

Forget exercise.

The word clearly doesn't sit well with you.

So let's talk about something you do every day without even thinking about it. Let's talk about your 'movement'. No, not your bowels. Let's build upon what you already do – and that's moving your body. But let's aim to do it a little more regularly and with more intentionality.

Let's focus on one aspect of movement in particular. Walking.

Now, if you're not able to walk for whatever reason then apply the same principles to a part of your body that you can move. So here's the idea. Over the years various gadgets from pedometers to smart watches have been able to track the number of steps we take. If you have a smartphone there may well be a health app on there that can do it.

I'm not quite sure if there's any real scientific literature to support 10,000 steps a day, but it seems to be a magic number many people aim for. Which is great, but not always achievable. Particularly if you're like my mum. Two knee replacements, a dodgy hip, and a walking stick, means 10,000 steps in a day is a big ask. It certainly won't be for everyone, but if you'll pardon the pun, it would be a step too far for my mum.

So let's make this idea both easy and motivating. Whatever the current number of steps you take each day (and if you haven't a clue, do something to enlighten yourself – I'm talking about your wellbeing and happiness here), your aim is simple. Increase the number of steps you take each year by 1 million.

Yep, that's it.

Told you it would be easy and motivating, didn't I?

And before you ask, no, I'm not kidding. I'm being deadly serious.

Increase the number of steps you take each year by *one million*.

Before you break out in a sweat at the mere thought of one million steps, trust me, it's easier than it sounds. It's just a simple task of breaking down what one million steps looks like over a year.

So let's do the maths. (And if you're reading this in America, yes, you read that correctly.)

In most years there are 365 days.

What figure do we need to multiply by 365 to get a total of one million?

2,740.

Actually that number will give you one hundred steps over a million.

Impressive eh?

An extra 2,740 steps a day adds up to over a million in a year.

Now let's break that down even further to emphasise just how doable that is.

Let's assume the average person is awake and active 16 hours a day. I realise how awake and how active may vary, but stick with me.

So how many steps would you need to do each hour to hit 2,740 a day?

One hundred and seventy-two.

That's it. No more.

One. Hundred. And. Seventy. Two.

What if that was still unrealistic for you to achieve for whatever reason?

OK. Let's aim for an extra half a million steps a year instead.

What does that break down to over an hour?

Eighty-six steps.

One of the big lessons I've learnt in life is that

> **there's magic in thinking big – but there's also motivation in starting small.**

Whether you aim for a million or half a million more steps there are two things you should know.

Your body will thank you.

You'll feel happier as a consequence.

I'd call that a result.

Changing Your Identity

In line with all the other tips in this chapter, here's another very small change that makes an enormous difference. Sometimes, in order to secure long-lasting permanent change, you have to change your identity. No, not literally. You don't have to march into the passport office and apply to be Dame Felicity Partington-Smyth, the Countess of Melbourne, distantly related to the Crown Prince of Ghana and 16th in line to the throne of the Ashanti people.

But you do have to switch your thinking and decide to be a new improved version of you.

It's subtle, but oh so powerful.

For example, shift your identity from thinking of yourself as 'someone who hates exercise' to 'I'm someone who looks after my physical health'. All of a sudden, walking, jogging and cycling make perfect sense. Yes, even on a rainy day when everyone else is being 'someone who makes excuses when it rains'.

Once you become that person and inhabit that way of thinking, looking after yourself becomes the most natural thing in the world. Exercise will start to become a natural part of your routine. Once you become the kind of person who looks after their physical wellbeing, the fast-food take-away becomes an occasional treat instead of a daily splurge.

The effort of diet and exercise melts away. They become the most natural things in the world.

Please note, this is about a million times more powerful than it sounds when you read it off the page – and here's the kicker: habits pass through families. For example, if your family members self-medicate with bad habits (overeat, drink excessively, binge-watch TV, etc.) you are likely to pick up those same behaviours. Basically, if your family doesn't care enough about their own health and wellbeing to change their behaviour, it can be harder for you to learn to love yourself enough to adopt a healthier lifestyle.

So here's your reminder. Close the book and take a look at the title. 'Revolution'. We're not inviting you to fall in line with everyone else. We're not asking you to do what's easiest. An invite to the happiness revolution is a challenge to step up, measure up and shape up. Break with the ranks. It doesn't matter what anyone else is doing, it matters what YOU are doing. Becoming someone who looks after their physical and mental health makes you a leader.

> **If habits run in families, this is a perfect opportunity to shape your own habits and set standards that will be followed for generations to come.**

In lockdown, I had some spare time and I invented some future binoculars. I'm peering through them right now. I can see the future you in the distance. In rude health. The future you is positively glowing. And, oh my goodness, I can see your great, great, great grandkids. They're amazing! They're waving madly. I'm trying to lip read… looks like they're shouting 'thank you'.

Find Your Full Stop

When you're reading a document, email, or a book, how do you know you've come to the end of a sentence?

Easy eh?

Because you'll come to a full stop.

That little dot is the writer's way of saying 'Have a break. Take a breath. Pause.' In fact, it might not only indicate the end of a sentence, but a paragraph, a chapter, or even the book. Either way, whatever the context, that full stop is indicating something has come to an end.

So here's my question.

What's your full stop?

What routine or ritual sends the message to your brain that your work has finished, it's time to have a break? To stop.

You see, some people's lives are lacking in full stops. There might be plenty of commas, even the odd hyphen, but their lives are lived at a relentless pace where they rarely switch off. They mistakenly believe that rest is the opposite of work.

Wrong.

Actually rest is not work's opposite – it's work's partner. In a nutshell,

to be at your best you need to rest.

In other words you need to stop and catch your breath. To pause. To allow your brain time to recharge (which is also why sleep is so important).

Checking emails on your phone while you're chilling with your partner on the couch is not rest. Finishing off an email on your laptop which is perched on your knee whilst you're watching TV in the evening is not a full stop.

The chances are that more of us are working from home. Previously the commute home was people's full stop. But what if your commute is a few metres' walk from one room to another? I'm aware that working from home can have many upsides – but don't ignore the downsides. Particularly if it begins to feel like you're living at work, rather than working from home.

So here's my question to you, whether or not you work from home: What do you do to let your brain know it's time to stop work for the day?

And if you don't have anything, find something.

You see, that is something that is in your control to do.

And who knows, with all that spare time, you might end up with 52 grandchildren.

Bonus tip

Can't sleep? Counting sheep is so boring (which is kind of why it works) but I find that counting my blessing works so much better. And just to spice it up, starting with A and working through to Z, you have to think of what you're grateful for, or lucky to have in your life.

Best. Game. Ever!

This is how my sleepless nights go…

Today I'm thankful to have anteaters in my life. I mean, just imagine how many ants there'd be in the world if there were no anteaters. We'd be literally overrun with ants. So anteaters, I salute you!

B? Belgium. Of all the countries beginning with 'B', Belgium is my all-time fave. It's a really nice country where they make the world's best chocolate. So, gosh, we're so lucky to live in a world where there's a country called Belgium.

Which makes C really easy – chocolate!

D is donkeys. Loveable, loyal, stubborn, hard-working and apparently you can boil them down to make glue. Donkeys. The ultimate multi-purpose animal.

I'm usually asleep by E. In fact, in all the times I've played the sleep blessings game, I've never made it past grapefruit.

Job done!

Make an Oath to Your Physical Self

Manifesto reminder

1 Focus on what you can control (clue: that's yourself, and not very much else).

2 Stop taking your health for granted. It's precious. Take care of it.

3 Eat, move and sleep are keystone habits. Get them right and everything else will seem a lot easier.

4 *True* self-care means looking after yourself now while also keeping an eye on the wellbeing of your future self.

5 Your body wants to be exercised. It'll thank you for it.

6 To make things easier, simply change your identity. Become *the kind of person who looks after their physical and mental health* and the effort melts away.

7 With work and home merging, the end of the working day needs acknowledging with a full-stop.

Life: The Small Print

Who reads terms and conditions? Even if you can be bothered, they're deliberately befuddling. 'Do tick the box if you don't want to receive no email contact'. Eh? What? Next day, the deluge of SPAM tells you the bastards nailed you. Again!

Ts & Cs comprise page after tedious page of boring get-outs and clauses that cause a glazing of the eyes. The worst thing is that you have no choice. Because the small print is now online, if you want to move on, you have to tick the box.

And so it was when your mum got pregnant with you. Before bringing you into the world, she had to sign up to God knows what. Do you think your mum went through every caveat, sub-clause and disclaimer? Of course she didn't. She was too busy painting the spare room and looking for a cot on Ebay.

Your mum signed up to the basic idea of birthing you – she signed you up to 'LIFE' – but she didn't scroll through the reams of small print. The old girl did what we all did, she scrolled through and ticked the *'I agree'* box at the end.

But we've unearthed the original document. We're not going to bore you with all 176 pages of small print, but it's worth reviewing the basic terms and conditions that come with the deal that we call 'LIFE'.

We thought you might like a few snippets of the original Ts & Cs:

1   'LIFE' comes with NO guarantees and absolutely NO refunds.

2   'LIFE' is not fair. (See clause 1.)

3   Grumbling that 'LIFE' is not fair is therefore true, but pointless.

4   'LIFE' comes with only one rule: *sometimes you just have to suck it up.* (See clauses 2 and 3.)

5   The length of 'LIFE' is variable. If you look after yourself you might experience an extended warranty. Note, *'might'*. (See clauses 1–4.)

6   The first few years of 'LIFE' are crucial but, even here, there are no guarantees. Your parents/guardians will be making it up as they go along. It's pot luck. (See clause 2.)

7 It is the user's responsibility to define what 'happiness' is for them. Note, this is highly variable. Some will find happiness in alcohol, others in purpose, some in countryside walks. Many will find happiness in shoes. Note: all are correct.

8 'LIFE' is a one-time thing. (For those banking on an afterlife, see clause 1.)

   i Finding happiness is the sole responsibility of the user.

   ii The management shall not be held responsible for the user failing to find happiness. (See clauses 1–7.)

9 What you make of 'LIFE' is totally up to you. (See clause 8.i.)

10 'LIFE' sometimes waits until you are down before kicking you in the teeth. (See clauses 2 and 5.)

11 'LIFE' is a contact sport. (See clause 10.)

12 'LIFE' is subject to change without notice.

13 'LIFE' is lived alongside other people who've also signed up to the exact same terms and conditions. When you look over your shoulder, their 'LIFE' contract might appear to be better than yours. It isn't and there are no 'swapsie deals'. (See clauses 1, 2, 3 and 9.)

14 'LIFE' is best lived loved. [1]

---

[1] From an original idea by Nigel Percy: currently the best writer to never have written a book
https://www.artofbrilliance.co.uk/meet-the-team/nigel-percy/

The Game of Life

Terms and conditions are one thing. The Game of LIFE also comes with rules.

I was born before computers had been invented. Instead of FIFA we played actual football with a 'casey'. On a wet day, the ball soaked up the water so when you headed it the imprint stayed on your forehead for the rest of the day.[2]

Our indoor games were Subbuteo, draughts and chess. These games involved skill and strategy, as well as a bit of luck. However, one game I played required no strategy – Snakes and Ladders. It was all down to the roll of the dice and the concentration levels of my opponent, as I was rather skilled at 'miscounting' the number of squares I had to move my counter in order to avoid landing on a snake. [Apologies. Yes, I was a cheat. See the earlier chapter on 'The Little Shop of Shame'.]

[2] If you're under 50, ask your dad about a 'casey' and you'll find we're correct.

It just so happens that life reminds me a little of Snakes and Ladders. I don't mean that everything that happens to us is down to chance – far from it – but sometimes, through no fault of our own, we might end up experiencing a 'snake event' in our lives. An unexpected challenge. Bad luck. An unfaithful partner. An awful boss. Redundancy. Ill health. A financial loss. Someone who cheats at board games.

I recognise that some challenges I've faced have been due to my poor choices, and I've needed to take responsibility when that's been the case. But sometimes it's not down to my poor choices. You see, although we might like to think we are the masters of our destiny – and I certainly believe we can influence it – some stuff that happens is out of our control.

We didn't choose our parents, siblings, the location we grew up in, or the time in history we were born. Similarly, we didn't choose to trigger the financial crisis of 2008 or unleash COVID-19 on a largely unsuspecting world. We don't choose floods, storms or other forces of nature. Nobody volunteers for cancer.

The reality is that some good people die young and some pretty awful people enjoy a long life. Some hard-working people still struggle financially (you don't see many nurses driving Ferraris) whilst some lazy people inherit large fortunes. It's a harsh pill to swallow, but quite a lot of what happens to us in life is sheer bad luck. It's more a matter of chance than choice.

So, if we are to be happy in life, we need to embrace an uncomfortable truth. The terms and conditions we parodied above – *they're true!*

Life. Is. Not. Fair.

People don't always get what they deserve. Seriously, they don't. And sometimes shit happens that no one sees coming. Yes, your misfortune is entirely undeserved and unwarranted but there's also an inevitability about it – at some point in the 'Board Game of Life' you will land on a snake. Sometimes you feel like Indiana Jones and being lowered into a pit of vipers: it's snake after snake after snake...

But here's the good news. It's a biggie, so pay attention.

The. Game. Isn't. Over.

Remember, when the cobras are hissing, the rattlers are rattling and the boas are constricting, you've still got the dice.

That means you're still in the game. Yes, there are snakes. I can't deny that. But remember this.

There are a few ladders on the board too.

Things can change.

And if you're open to the idea, I reckon there are times when we might just be able to load the dice slightly in our favour. Is there a formula that will guarantee landing on a ladder every time? Nope.

BUT... (and it's another of our big BUTs) there are strategies, insights, ideas, pearls of wisdom backed by science that do significantly improve our chances of success, happiness, and landing on some of those ladders.

If there's one fundamental life truth I have learnt it's this: you can't always influence the event, but you can choose how you respond to it. David Taylor calls it the gap of infinite possibilities. It's about grasping the fact that events don't necessarily lead to inevitable outcomes. Life is a little messier and more fluid than a maths equation. A setback for one person that sees them quit is a stepping-stone for someone else that sees them press on.

Same event. Different outcome.

Life is a major event. It's the most important board game you'll ever play. Life can be an experience that is taken for granted and wasted, or an opportunity to be seized and lived to the full. So that serious stuff that could screw up your life could,
in hindsight, be the best thing that could ever have happened to you.

That struggle you've wrestled with could actually strengthen you.

That disappointment that could have led to despair has in fact deepened your resolve to appreciate your life and given you the determination to persevere.

So yes, life is about tales of the unexpected. Bad stuff does happen. A random roll of the dice may land you on a snake. You can throw your hands up and complain. You can bemoan your lot: *it always happens to me!* You can tip the board up and storm off to your bedroom because *'it's a stupid game anyway'*. In the context of the Game of Life, when shit happens our go-to strategy might be to reach for our freshly ironed victim t-shirt.

But sometimes we also need to acknowledge that setbacks, disappointments, heartbreaks and struggle are all woven into the fabric of life. No matter how hard we try they cannot be avoided, and we place our happiness in a highly vulnerable position if we think it can only be achieved when there's an absence of pain and struggle in our lives.

Or, when you encounter a snake you can choose to roll with it. By 'rolling with it' I mean rolling up your sleeves and rolling the dice again. Perhaps one of the most important things to realise about happiness is this – it's not the absence of struggle; it's not a state you only experience when you're worry and problem free. Sometimes it's quite the opposite.

> **Fulfilment and a sense of achievement come from successfully meeting challenges – not from constantly avoiding them.**

Believe me, it's not the easy life you're after. Seriously, it's not. Imagine for a moment that to avoid anyone's hurt feelings, we eliminate the snakes from the board. You'd ask your family, 'Who's up for a game of ladders and ladders?' and I guarantee no takers. 'What's the point?' they'd say. 'It's so boring.' If there are no snakes, no challenges and no setbacks there is no chance of winning against the odds.

You see, this might sound counterintuitive, but 'the easy life' can quickly turn into 'the boring life'. Our ancestors didn't evolve and put us at the top of the food chain because everything was handed to them on a plate. We learnt to compete and collaborate *because* of challenge – not because of its absence. We buy into the myth that people can only be happy when things are going well, when life is perfect. Whereas the truth is something quite different.

Here's the deal. There is another way: when bad stuff happens it's a case of developing a backbone instead of a wishbone. In other words, don't just go through the experience but *grow* through it. To become better people, not broken, bitter shadows of our former selves. Resilience is about knowing that the route to happiness and fulfilment is often about taking the less trodden path. That means persevering, giving things a go, being open to challenges and getting gritty. Building these mental muscles puts you in a better place to deal with the world as it is, not the world as you want it to be.

Best of all, happiness isn't about rainbows and unicorns. It's not about dodging pain and eliminating suffering. It's about learning to handle LIFE and all its ridiculous subclauses much better – to make room for emotional lows, reduce their impact, and create a flourishing life *despite* it never quite being how you want it.

Our thinking is this: if a bit of shit's good for the roses, it might just be good for us too. There's no silver bullet or quick fix answer, but here are a couple of ideas that will help you turn the bad stuff into fertiliser for personal growth.

Learn the Lessons

If you ever feel sad, just remember: even unicorns probably have diarrhoea every once in a while.

You know that widely quoted phrase 'everything happens for a reason'? Well let me let you into a secret. Sometimes the reason is… you!

Seriously it is.

It's the dumb-ass decision you made. It's the email you sent when you were angry. It was your propensity to act first and think later. It was due to your stubbornness which, bizarrely, you talk about as if it's a medical condition you're unable to change. It's your not wanting to cause offence, then letting people walk over you. It's your tendency to procrastinate and avoid taking action in case you fail. It's the fact you've taken your loved ones for granted for too long…

How do we know? Because the previous paragraph was written about your authors. Remember, we're human too! Let's be honest. Some of the bad stuff we've experienced has been manufactured by ourselves. Now please re-read that last sentence and notice I said 'some'. However, whether we like it or not, the fact remains that *some* of our anguish is self-created.

So rather than invite some friends round to play the BSE game – Blame Someone Else – you might want to start by taking a look in the mirror first. The mirror you've brushed your teeth into twice daily since you grew teeth, we call it the mirror of personal responsibility. It's amazing, but when you take responsibility for your personal actions and accept you may have played at least a contributory role in things not turning out right, you're in a much better position to move on and make manure.

Of course, our get-out clause appeared earlier in the chapter. Sometimes what happened was out of your control. Life threw you a curveball. You were unlucky. Sometimes it does seem like there are snakes around every corner. So I'm not going to pretend it's easy, but trust me, there's always a lesson to learn from our experiences, no matter how difficult that may be.

We often think resilience is solely about the ability to recover from a setback. But sometimes we need to ask ourselves why the setback happened in the first place.

> **It's not always simply about your ability to recover from a fall – it's also about understanding why you fell in the first place.**

So don't lose the lesson. What you go through you can grow through. Believe me. I've had to make a lot of manure over the years.

#Bemorehippo

Top tip:
Conventional wisdom suggests that if you're angry you should 'count to 10' which allows the red mist to evaporate. Research suggests that once the source of anger is removed your emotion system returns to normal after about 20 minutes. So, top emotional intelligence tip, don't count to 10 when you're mad, count to 1,200!

With Subbuteo, Snakes and Ladders and The Game of Life already referenced, we move adroitly to Hungry Hippos. My hippo factsheet tells me that these 'river cows' have pink sweat, which acts as sunblock. Also, I discover that they're herbivores so they don't eat people, but they do charge at people, so stay clear of a hungry hippo. Best of all, they have eyes, ears and nose on the top of their heads so they can immerse themselves in the river yet still look and listen and breathe. I experimented in the bath last night and can safely report that humans aren't arranged for that to happen. I nearly drowned trying.

The hippo factsheet also tells us what we already know: the river cows adore mud. They wallow. It's useful. It helps them cool down. And I think there should be a human equivalent. Languishing in the mire is fine. It's useful. You can actually enjoy a wallow. The trick is to know when and how to get out of the mire.

Although it's not easy, it's perfectly possible to develop some mental muscles. Think about it. Loads of adults go to the gym to work on their *physical* strength. Some want to tone their bodies, develop some biceps, maybe get a tummy six-pack. But it's also perfectly possible to develop *mental* strength – an emotional six-pack – a set of resilience skills that will allow you to cope with the weight of the world.

And while most books will expand on what mental toughness is, it's worth reflecting on what it absolutely isn't. Mental toughness is *not* about pretending things are okay when they're not. Neither is it about supressing negative feelings, or hiding them. It's also not about beating yourself up or winning at all costs.

So #BeMoreHippo. Have some downtime. It's okay to have a bad day.

Being authentically human is absolutely not about being happy all the time.

Sure, being happy is a great feeling – but ALL the time? In my school sessions I sometimes pose a question to the kids: I hold up a small box and say 'Imagine that inside this box is a pill. And if you take the pill, it'll make you happy forever.'

They look excited.

'Yes, one pill will make you 100% happy for the rest of your life.' I ask the kids, 'Who'd take the pill?'

There's normally a rush of hands. 'Hell yeah. Happiness, bring it on!'

But I can always rely on a sceptic who will kick off a discussion. 'What – *always?*' they will ask with a healthy tone of inquiry. 'In *every* situation?'

I'll nod. 'Yep, always happy, guaranteed, for the rest of your life.'

Another kid will then pipe up. 'What about, like, funerals and stuff?'

'*Especially* at funerals and stuff,' I say, hamming it up.

'And when I lose a football match, or do badly on a test?'

'Absolutely,' I say. 'Just one little pill.'

Of course, by now, most hands have gone down. 'Being happy at a funeral wouldn't be right,' someone will say. 'Being sad would be better.'

'And if I was happy about losing the match, I'd have no incentive to improve. Same with being happy about flunking the test.'

And bit by bit the young people come to realise that there's a massive range of emotions, all of which are perfectly okay. Even the ones that feel really horrible are okay because they kick you into action. The important thing is to understand what these emotions are telling you, and to take positive action as a result. Delivering workshops in schools is always seat of the pants stuff but usually the discussion ends up with them working it out for themselves. They'll tell me that mental strength is often about sitting with these difficult emotions and making sense of them. They'll realise that difficult emotions sometimes lead to difficult decisions and that mental strength is about having the courage to stand up for what's right. A school audience will figure that it's absolutely about knowing what your values are and living by them. It's about knowing what mark you want to make on the world and setting about making it. It's about having a positive mindset, learning from failure, making good choices (consistently) and spending your energy wisely. Moreover, children and young people will begin to realise that just because they've messed up doesn't mean they are messed up.

> **I enrolled for a class in 'Dealing with Disappointment' – but the teacher never showed up.**

Which is where hippo time comes in. In order to recover from a setback we need first to allow ourselves time to acknowledge its impact on us. To give ourselves time to explore how we're feeling. Denying that we're hurt or in pain is not helpful.

It's unhealthy to supress your hurt. You need to process it and then find a way to express it.

Vent. Shout. Scream. Blame the universe. Avoid cats in case you kick them, though. But when shit happens, be real. If you need to grieve over something, do so. Pretending to be happy is a lousy strategy. It's counterintuitive I know, but giving yourself time to process your pain is a powerful way to come to terms with it. Superficial, fake cheery smiles painted on with the brush of denial aren't.

But here's a warning. Hippo time is okay, but it's temporary. It's a necessary and important part of your journey, but please take a moment to digest this next point.

It. Is. Not. Your. Destination.

Process your pain. Sit with your sadness. Digest your disappointment. It's all part of your recovery.

You'll be stronger as a result, trust me. Just make sure that whatever you've gone through ultimately leaves you better, not bitter.

Bitterness will break you.

So my very best advice for pledge #4 is this. LIFE's terms and conditions are what they are. Events will be what they will be.

> Life never claimed to be fair so when shit inevitably happens, make manure, not war.

Commit to Acknowledging the Small Print

Manifesto reminder

1 Life comes with terms and conditions, most of which are loaded against you. If you think it's not fair, you are 100% correct. But it is what it is.

2 Life's a game of Snakes and Ladders. You will sometimes roll bad dice and find yourself back to square one. See point 1 above.

3 You might feel down, but you're not out. The fat lady hasn't sung. You're still in the game. Roll again. Remember, *look for the ladders!*

4 It's okay to not be okay. Have some hippo time. Enjoy your wallow. But don't spend too long in the mud or it'll set hard in the African sun and you'll never get out!

MANIFESTO PLEDGE #5

PROMISE TO VALUE YOUR VALUES

Advance warning: pledges 5 and 6 are joined at the hip. Grab a brew and a biscuit and read them in one sitting.

There's an awful lot written about goal setting, with our emphasis on *awful*. We've done our level best to make sure this isn't that. Our aim is to distil the wisdom of goal setting down into pledges 5 and 6 so they become the definitive chapters.

No bull. No fluff. No nonsense. We want these to be the only chapters on goal setting you ever need.

Hence pledges 5 and 6 have levels. They build into something quite thrilling but you need four essentials before you venture any further.

First, a hard hat. Paul gets a bit in yer face.

Second, that fire in your belly, blow on the embers. You're going to need to find some passion.

The third essential is an open mind. One thing I've learned over the years is that the trouble with having an open mind is that people keep coming along and trying to put things in it. Which is exactly what we'll be attempting to do.

And lastly, you'll need a head for heights because when you get to our top level, it's nosebleed territory.

Those four things. Got them? Blow on those embers. Excellent. Onwards...

Bjorn Again

To achieve level 1, you need to play our game of 'Pick a Winner'. In the list below, simply tick your preferred option:

PICK A WINNER!

☐ Orange flavour or an actual orange? ☐

☐ Freshly ground coffee or instant? ☐

☐ Sean Connery or any other Bond? ☐

□ Mr Whippy or Ben and Jerry's? □

□ Fresh or tinned salmon? □

□ Olives eaten on holiday in Tuscany,
or on your pizza in Aldershot? □

□ A postcard or the actual holiday? □

□ A paperback or a Kindle? □

□ Genuine customer care or a *have a nice day* smile? □

□ That 'When Harry met Sally' moment or a real orgasm? □

□ Abba or Bjorn Again? □

□ Sunday lunch with your family or a chicken dinner ready
meal for one? □

□ The Serengeti or West Midlands Safari Park? □

□ The Eiffel Tower or Blackpool Tower? □

□ A trip to see Santa in Lapland or in a department store? □

□ Monet's original 'Water Lilies' above your fireplace, or a print
from IKEA? □

Our simple tick box exercise brings us onto mashed potato...

Instant mashed potato. Just add hot water to some chemical granules and hey presto – wa minute later you've got yourself a plate of fake food.

Replace 'nourishing and tasty' with 'quick and easy' and we're slap bang into another metaphor about life.

The problem with *real* mashed potato is that it requires time and effort. You've got to plant seeds and grow spuds. Then there's waiting and picking and peeling and boiling and mashing and a nob of butter and a dash of cream and a pinch of salt, whereas the instant is, well, effortless.

But easy success tastes synthetic. It doesn't satisfy. It isn't nourishing. You may get success served on a plate, but it won't fulfil you. You'll still have an empty feeling.

You see, it's not just achieving your goal that makes you happy. It's the journey it took to get there.

It's the struggle. The setbacks. It's about how you grew because of what you went through. That's what counts.

In the real or fake tick boxes above, we're guessing that, by and large, you'll prefer the genuine article. There's only one *real* Santa, right? The real McCoy is preferable to the doppelganger.

Let go of aiming for perfection. It's much more satisfying and fulfilling to be authentically human. With that in mind we'd like to park the watered-down version of you right here and invite the 100% genuine everyday superhero you to step forward into level 2 . . .

The Grand Slam Values Challenge

Top tip:
Stop trying to
be 'all that' and
start being 'all
you'

Life is a game of compare and contrast. Like it or not, there's a pecking order and we all suss where we fit in. Again, like it or not, we aspire to be at the top of the totem pole because we judge the top dogs to have achieved 'success' which is, more often than not, measured by status, wealth, and power.

However, it's quite easy to get so caught up in earning money, furthering our careers and cultivating 'followers' that we neglect our health and family.

There's a huge point that I'm side-stepping because it necessitates a book of its own but it boils down to this: you can be a low dog on the financial totem pole and yet still be hugely successful, if you dare to measure 'success' in non-traditional terms. If true wealth is measured by 'happiness' and 'contentment', I promise you, many of the top dogs might score high on 'material wealth' but at the expense of human happiness.

That point is deliberately parked because we have another game for you.

Gandhi, Mandela, Pankhurst, Jobs, Trump, Hitler: they all had goals. Maybe the top tip from them is to make sure you're driven by the *right* things.

Values are like a compass. They will guide you but you will stray. Sometimes you might get a little lost. Which is fine. Life has many paths. There are right ways, wrong ways and in-between ways. It's confusing and everyone loses their way sometimes. When you feel lost, consult your values once more. They will bring you back on track.

So here's an activity that's guaranteed to help you rekindle your internal fire as well as point you in the right direction. In the values tennis tournament, you get to choose the winner in each round. It's *so, so* difficult but well worth the mental effort.

Choose wisely...

Typically, we aren't that closely connected with our values, and because of that, we can easily get caught up in goals that are not truly meaningful to us. We're advocating a values-focused approach to goal setting. Yes, we set goals, because goals are essential to a fulfilling, rewarding life, but if we align them with our values they become a lot more personally meaningful.

Let's take a simple example. Suppose you have the long-term goal of retraining to be a teacher. The training will take some time, and we'd hate for you to spend the next year of your life doggedly focused on that goal, thinking you can't be fulfilled until you've achieved it. So ask yourself, *what is this goal in the service of? What will it enable me to do that's truly meaningful?*

We're mad keen that you enjoy the achievement **AND** the twists and turns along the way. Sometimes the light at the end of the tunnel will seem an awfully long way off. In our values challenge, your final 4 will light the way.

VALUES CHALLENGE

My final 4:

Friendship
Competitive
Resilient
Belonging
Dedication
Fun
Taking Risks
Teamwork
Winning
Reliable
Loved
Loving
Gratitude
Learning
Excited
Calm

Hard Working
Proud
Kind
Responsible
Respectful
Ambitious
Realistic
Optimistic
Fair
Enthusiastic
Confident
Famous
Adventurous
Forgiving
Brave
Creative

Promise to Value Your Values

Manifesto reminder

1 It's easy to live a fake life. THE HAPPINESS REVOLUTION requires you to step into your best self. Drop the pretence. Be authentically 100% you.

2 Spend some time working out what you stand for. Your values will light the way.

MANIFESTO PLEDGE #6

DARE TO STAND OUT BY BEING MUCH LESS SMART

Aim. Fire. Ready.

'NEVER GIVE UP. Unless you've tried at least 3 times cos then it's just impossible.' #pewdiepie

Have you ever been a member of a club or society?

As a small child my mum thought it would be a good idea to send me to dance school. I was the only boy in the class. I was less Billy Elliot and more Billy Idiot. I will probably go down in the record books as being the youngest person ever to master the art of 'dad dancing'.

Then came my teenage years. Not wanting my lack of talent to hold me back, I joined drama school and I'm proud to say that those skills have never left me. I'm still pretty good at creating a drama. If you want someone to make a scene, I'm your man.

I was also a member of the school chess club. Captain, no less! Which sounds super-impressive until I tell you that the club only had one member. Me against me, there was only ever going to be one captain and one winner. My commitment to attending solo chess club was fuelled by the fact that I was 13 and smitten. I fancied Mrs Perry who ran it.

Recently I thought about setting up my own members-only 'Procrastinators' Club', but never got round to it.

If you smiled reading that last sentence, the world needs more people like you.

But it is actually worth thinking, if such a club existed, how many people who actually needed it would attend? My guess is most people would find an excuse not to be there – although procrastinators rarely use the word 'excuse' – they're much more comfortable with the word 'reason'.

That's actually something I've noticed about myself and other people – most of us are rather adept at justifying our lack of action.

Procrastination has become an art form. As the modern meme says: *I used to be a crastinator, but then I went pro.*

Why is that?

Well, actually admitting to the real reason we don't do things can be difficult. Being honest with ourselves and others can be uncomfortable. There's a lot of squirming in your seat. In chemistry and physics there's something called activation energy – the initial burst of energy that's required to break the inertia. Yes, it seems that even molecules can't really be bothered until they're energised. In human language, we cultivate excuses. Cutting to the chase, it's easier to put things off.

In my experience,

> **if you really want to do something you find a way – and if you don't, you find an excuse.**

Membership of Procrastinators' Club is swelled by the fact that our brains aren't bothered about whether we've got a lofty long-term project in mind. Safety, survival and sex are its main priorities. Once these basics are satiated we move onto to seeking belonging and love. Tick those and we can begin to pursue longer-term ambitions.

But these so-called lower-order needs can dominate. Most people have tacit goals. Quietly, in their heads, their aim is to 'get through the week' or 'survive till my next holiday'. This is incredibly common and sadly you fall into the trap of accidentally wishing your life away.

Those who do set goals often set them badly. Most people intuitively know that having a goal (or goals) will motivate them but the closest they get is setting a lame New Year's Resolution and life plays out as

Groundhog Year: January 1st sees a burst of enthusiasm for a 'new improved you' with all hope dashed by January 4th. You then spend 361 days in one of the comfy chairs at Procrastinators' Club while you wait for January 1st to roll around for another try.

The magic doesn't happen inside the oak-panelled walls of a cosy club. Our ability to try new things shouldn't be something that reaches its sell-by date when we turn 50. But you will be tempted! As you mature, it's easy to confuse comfort with happiness. Adventure, risk, trying new things, being curious and creative – that's all well and good while you're finding your way in life. But you reach a point where comfort and predictability make more sense.

Don't get me wrong. Being comfortable is appealing. I quite like a bit of predictability and routine. But do you know what? Too much of it can make you stale.

There's a difference between 'being alive' and 'truly living'. You know this to be true and, on the one hand, life is bellowing at you every day, *'Hey you, isn't being alive amazing? What shall we do to experience the incredible privilege of living on this planet?'* And yet you can be deaf to the message. It's easy to become stuck in our cage of comfort, oblivious to the clarion call, because we've got our headphones on, listening to the same song on repeat.

The pandemic fell under the heading of 'big life events' that slap you in the face like a wet flannel. With hindsight you begin to realise that 'lockdown' was a metaphor for life. Ensnared in your comfort zone it dawns on you that there's nobody else you can blame. You were locked down way before actual lockdown and worse still, it was you who locked yourself down. Now where the hell did I leave the key?

We all need our cage of comfort rattled occasionally, otherwise we can develop life's equivalent of bed sores. We can get so comfortable that it can become uncomfortable. We realise that if we risk nothing, we are in fact risking everything.

Our advice is to quit waiting for the perfect time. Rarely is it a case of *ready, aim, FIRE!* There are always too many ducks to line up. Waiting until everything is just right, for the perfect time and conditions, means you'll be finding more excuses *not* to take action. 'I'll just attend two more meetings of Procrastinators' Club and then I'll do something.'

Yawn.

Meantime, the doers are doing. They broke the rules. They went *aim, FIRE, ready* or *FIRE, ready, aim* or any other combination thereof. Our point is that the doers almost certainly weren't ready. They didn't really know if they were doing the right things, but they did them anyway. And no matter how slow their progress, I promise you they'll be moving faster than those who are chewing the fat and sipping sour milk down at Procrastinators' Club.

Here's some tough love. You ain't going to live for ever, so how about you quit the excuses, park the complacency, resign your membership of Procrastinators' Club, and get on with living rather than simply existing.

You've got a contribution to make. You've got something to give. I've not got the slightest clue what it is, because I don't know you. But deep down you know. You know we weren't meant to doze and drift through our days here. We weren't designed simply to enjoy an easy, comfortable life with no challenge or struggle. We were designed to grow, to explore, to experience, to enjoy.

To *do*.

Not just fantasise.

Not just dream.

Not just talk.

But to actually '*do*'.

> **'A little less conversation and a little more action.'** [Elvis]

To make the magic happen – whatever that magic is for you. Settling is okay, so long as you're settling for 'extraordinary'. Anything less and you've sold yourself short. My motivational speech can be summed up as only a northerner can: *get off your arse and start living your life.* (Note to my co-author: that's the potential book title, right there!)

My plea is actually very simple and from the heart. Get started. Do something.

Don't wait to feel motivated. You could be waiting a long time.

And the feelings fade anyway. Sometimes it's just about showing up.

With that off my chest, good news, you've qualified for our highest level of goal setting…

There's Just One Rule of Goal-Setting Club

If you've mastered the art of goal setting – that is, you have goals, they motivate you and you are propelled forward by them – we doff our metaphorical caps to you. Please skip this section.

For the vast majority who struggle or are confused by the whole goal conundrum, stick with us. Level 1 hinted that you need to be the authentic you. You're not interested in faking an epic life, you're determined to create a proper one. That means knowing what your values are and leaning into them.

Hopefully the previous section encouraged you to give up your membership of the cosy club. Yet you can do those things and **STILL** fail because when it comes to setting goals the only rule is: **THERE ARE NO RULES!**

We have a couple of points of advice that you'd do well to heed but, other than that, it's freestyle.

In the good advice column we'd suggest that you don't set a dead person's goal. By that, I mean never set as your goal as something that a dead person can do better than you. For example, to *stop* eating cake or chocolate – that's something a dead person can do better than you because, no matter what, they'll definitely never, ever eat cake again. Or to *stop* hitting the snooze button, or to *quit* smoking, or *stop* being negative.

Any goal that is about *not* doing something or *stopping* doing something is a dead person's goal. To convert it to a live person's goal you need to ask yourself, 'If I was no longer doing this activity (or feeling this way or thinking like this), what would I be doing with my time?'

For example, suppose you answered, 'If I was no longer scoffing cake, I'd be eating fruit instead', make that your goal. 'To eat 5 pieces of fruit and veg every day' is something that leaves a dead person in your wake.

In the same vein, 'If I wasn't smoking I'd be going for a brisk walk in the fresh air' and **BOOM**, you've left the dead person eating dust.

If I *wasn't* being negative and self-critical, if I *wasn't* hitting snooze, if I *wasn't* drinking wine every single night... we'll let you work out the positive alternatives for yourself.

Next up, be a little bit risky. Hey, I want to limit the damage to my self-esteem too – so I get where people are coming from. But

**your self-esteem isn't protected by never taking a risk.
It's built by taking chances.**

And that means sometimes falling flat on your face and still having the courage to get back up and try again. That's how your self-esteem grows – when you realise you're OK, even when everything doesn't go OK.

Take it from me, it's okay to fail and it's quite sexy to look a bit silly.[1] Now don't get me wrong, I'm not encouraging reckless, impulsive action. It's not a case of action at all costs. Keep your brain engaged at all times. Seek advice from others. Get feedback. We all need a support team. Sometimes we need people to tell us when we're making stupid decisions, but we also need people who can help us develop a strategy on how to achieve what we're trying to do.

On occasions your most important action is just to listen. But you're listening to learn and then do something with your learning.

And please remember this. Success isn't straight. Progress isn't steady and linear. Success looks rather like a plate of spaghetti bolognaise. It's difficult to know exactly where to start and finish. With spag bol, you just stick your fork in, whirl it around and slurp some in.

Yes, success is messy!

Our third piece of sage goal-setting advice is to ditch the tried, trusted and terribly bland **SMART** objectives mantra. If you already know what **SMART** stands for, our advice is to unlearn it. If you've never heard of **SMART**, congratulations. We're not going to trot it out here.

Some people will be wincing at our **SMART**-bashing. Corporate types will have had SMART beaten into them. Every workshop you've ever been on, every target you've ever set, every appraisal you've ever been to, every sales meeting … *hishhhhhhhh* … that's the sound of **SMART** being branded into your corporate hide.

----

[1] Check out the so-called 'pratfall effect': Helmreich, R., Aronson, E., & LeFan, J. (1970). To err is humanizing sometimes: Effects of self-esteem, ability, and a pratfall on interpersonal attraction. *Journal of Personality and Social Psychology*, 16(2), 259.

Just because everyone else has the same branding doesn't mean it's right. Our advice is to look around at the living dead **AND NOT BECOME ONE**. Bottom line? I cannot think of a single breakthrough in humankind that would ever have been achieved with a **SMART** objective. Ditch **SMART** and your life will be easier because you're not rising from the utterly bland starting point of having your dreams smashed by mediocrity.

Quitting **SMART** is top advice, but in favour of what?

Tissues at the ready. We're entering nosebleed territory...

Goal-Setting Madness

> **'We may encounter many defeats but we must not be defeated.'**
> **[Maya Angelou]**

Be authentic, tune into your values, quit Procrastinators' Club and ditch **SMART** objectives. *Yadda yadda yadda.*

What about the goal-setting process itself? Should they be big, small, short term, long term, career based... if starting is crucial, **HOW** do I start?

Feeling fired up is great, but please don't think that taking action will suddenly change your life. Aiming high is great. But start small. Baby steps are fine to begin with. Maybe the first step is to be clear on what you want to achieve – and more importantly, why you want to do it. Don't do something because you think it's what's expected of you. Don't do it because it will impress others.

That's not the point.

> **It's your life so do something you know will fulfil you. It doesn't have to be dramatic and daring. It might even appear boring to other people.**

Again, that's not the point.

It's *your* magic. You're making the most of the privilege of life. You're making the most of the opportunities your grandparents and the hundred or so billion people who've been here before you could not even have dreamed of.

Don't underestimate the importance of small daily steps. Don't be disappointed or disillusioned by the lack of instant, overnight success. That rarely, if ever, happens. As James Clear, author of the brilliant book *Atomic Habits*, says, 'Be impatient with your actions but patient with your results.'

You're playing the long game. You're not just dreaming it – you're taking action.

But there's still something missing. Achieving goals is a mix of will power and way power. Knowing where you're heading is important, but when things get messy, what then? It can be so tempting to re-enrol at Procrastinators' Club. If you walk by and peer in the window you'll see the same familiar faces, drinking the same sour milk, making the same excuses. The club looks oh so comfy. Your seat is empty. It's as if they've been expecting you back.

To tap into your will and way power, I'm convinced you should go large. In modern parlance, you should supersize your goals. I've heard it called the Law of GOYA (Get Off Your Ass). Check out the pyramid. It's based on an idea introduced to us by our goal-setting guru mate, David Hyner.[2]

To kickstart your ambition you need to set a Huge Unbelievably Great Goal, something that excites you, an achievement that is on the edges of your ability. You won't achieve your **HUGG** by next week or next month and certainly not by accident.

---

[2] David Hyner's website: https://www.stretchdevelopment.com/

The Happiness Revolution

It goes at the top of the pyramid. It doesn't just whet your appetite, it drenches it in motivation. It's a bit bonkers but once you've written your Huge Unbelievably Great Goal at the top of the pyramid it's the equivalent of burning your Procrastinators' Club membership card.

Clue: If your **HUGG** doesn't excite you, you've not framed it right.

The **HUGG** can seem daunting. It's so big and so thrilling – where the heck do I start? The answer was provided by my co-author a few sentences ago. The massive goal is broken down into smaller, more manageable steps. Each block of the HUGG becomes a **SUGG** – a set of *Small* Unbelievably Great Goals – things you are going to have to do every single day.[3]

Fill the whole thing in and you've got an exciting vision to aim for plus a host of small habits to commit to.

> '**I really think a champion is defined not by their wins, but by how they can recover when they fall.**'
> **[Serena Williams]**

[3] From an original idea by the remarkable Martin Burder: https://www.artofbrilliance.co.uk/meet-the-team/martin-burder/

There you have it in all its simplicity. No bull. No fluff. Ladies and gents, we give you **HUGGs** and **SUGGs**. They'll take you one step beyond.

It's goal-setting madness.

Dare to Stand Out by Being Much Less Smart

Manifesto reminder

1 Don't be misled by 'ready, aim, fire'. If you're waiting for the ideal moment or the perfect opportunity, you'll probably die waiting.

2 The team at Procrastinators' Club have always got a deal on. It's always the exact same 'free lifetime membership' deal. However tempting it sounds, don't join. If you have joined, burn your membership card. NOW!

3 Don't set a dead person's goal. The dead person will always beat you (and that's embarrassing).

4 Success is messy. Get yourself caked in messiness.

5 Ditch SMART goals. Go large. Set yourself a Huge Unbelievably Great Goal (or goals).

6 Break your HUGG into Small Unbelievably Great Goals. SUGGs will take you one step beyond.

Top Relationship tip:
Hold your viewpoint lightly. Make
room for new perspectives.

Around the World in 80 Words

I'm besotted with language.

'Rats live on no evil star' is my school starter and once kids get it, they're with me on a literary luge of thrills, spills and ridiculousness.

I wriggled with glee when I discovered that *hippopottomonstrosesqui-pedaliophobia* is the fear of long words. Some of my favourite obscure and/or slang British words are *basorexia* (the sudden urge to kiss someone) and *pronoia* (the opposite of paranoia – a strange, creeping feeling that everyone is out to *help* you).

We all know that Eskimos have umpteen words for the different types of snow. Sad as it may sound, I learned them! Check out my favourites – they are almost poetic: *oppas* (untouched, untrodden snow), *ceeyvi* (snow hardened by the wind to such a degree that reindeer cannot forage through it for food), *soavli* (wet, slushy snow) and *moarri* (condition of snow whose crust breaks and cuts the legs of reindeer moving through it).

To illustrate how language is shaped by your environment, the Zimbabweans (not big on snow) have a similar lexicon of words, but for walking. Check these delicious examples where a single word sums an entire style of walking: *dowor* (walk for a long time on bare feet), *chakwair* (walk making a squelching noise through mud), *minair* (walk with swinging hips), and my all-time favourite *mbwembwer* (walk with the buttocks shaking about).

Find your *mbwembwer* swagger. That's a top feelgood tip, right there.

My self-indulgent Inuit and Zimbabwean introduction brings me onto a smorgasbord of words (see what I did there?) from across the globe. Some might seem silly, all are meaningful, some deeply profound. I've followed some of them up with deeper explanation and top tips, whilst others are left for you to mull.

Please mull long and hard. Say the words out loud as you read them. Drop the funny ones into everyday conversation, but most of all enjoy, learn and live by the ones you find most profound.

Your Catalytic Converter

We all live in the real world. No matter how positive you are there will be days when your get-up-and-go has got up and gone. In which case the Breton language (very much an endangered species, spoken in south-western France) has the perfect word; *startijen*. It's the kick of energy you get from a strong cup of coffee or opening your curtains onto a sunny morning. It initiates action. *Startijen* is your kickstart.

Here's a top *startijen* life hack, the catalyst that will shake you from inertia, courtesy of the marvellous Mel Robbins.[1] The 5-second rule is the simplest concept in the entire book. The only skill you require is to be able to count backwards from 5 to 1.

Example: sometimes the alarm goes and I really don't feel like getting out of bed. Especially when it's dark outside and I have things to do that don't excite me. It's easier to have a sneaky lie in, an extra half an hour. On the one hand, it's perfectly fine to treat myself to a cheeky lie-in – *sometimes* – but if I do it too often it sends my day out of kilter. With no time for breakfast, I'd leave the house in a hurry, rushing to wherever I'm supposed to be, getting caught in the rush hour, I'd forget my lunch, or my phone… once I was so rushed I forgot to put my shoes on and rocked up to work in my slippers. I guess it could have been worse – at least I was wearing a suit and not my Hulk onesie.

But my extra 30 minutes in bed had made me feel a bit like the Hulk. I'd end up playing catch-up all day, rushed, stressed, on edge and angry with myself.

---

[1] Robbins, M. (2017). *'The 5 Second Rule: The Surprisingly Simple Way to Live, Love, and Speak with Courage: Transform your Life, Work, and Confidence with Everyday Courage.* New York: Post Hill Press.

Mel's 5-second rule has been astonishingly helpful. Whilst acknowledging an important part of self-care is to allow myself an *occasional* lie in, they are no longer a habit. On those mornings when my mojo has gone AWOL, instead of rolling over and going back to sleep I count down – 5, 4, 3, 2, 1 – and launch myself out of bed.

Mel swears by it and I can see why. It just works.

Your brain is very good at finding excuses for you NOT to do things. Whenever an event happens that requires you to take an action you know you should take, but don't want to, time begins to pass while you mull it over.

Humans are the animal kingdom's best over-thinkers.

The longer you leave it before taking action (the longer the gap of over-thinking time), the more likely it is that the gap gets filled with dread, anxiety, self-doubt and negativity or good old fashioned things called EXCUSES. Those feelings settle in, get the better of you and you talk yourself into NOT doing whatever it is you could/should have been doing.

In my 'getting out of bed' example, if I think about it for too long my brain will come up with lots of reasons why staying in bed is the best option. *It's so warm and snuggly in here and, besides, an extra half an hour won't hurt. In fact, it might do you good. And you can skip breakfast… I mean, who needs breakfast anyway, it's so over-rated…* and before you know it, you've nodded off and you're running late.

The 5-second rule cuts the thinking gap. The alarm goes and BOOM, 5 seconds later you're out of bed and ready for action. Feet planted, sleep wiped from your eyes, you're a readiness ninja. Your brain is like

'Wow, no messin'. You mean ACTION, baby'.

It's not just about waking up in the morning. The event happens [alarm goes off, speak up in a meeting, start some exercise, clean your bathroom, get your yoga mat out, ask someone out…] and if you give yourself too much time to think, you talk yourself out of it.

Your mind is an amazing piece of kit, but remember Procrastinators' Club from earlier? The cosiest club in the world, where everyone has complimentary lifetime membership. It's always open. And there's a comfy excuses chair right there by the fire where you can sip your sour milk and have a chin wag with all the other non-doers.

Remember, your brain is brilliant at inventing all sorts of wonderfully plausible excuses [too tired/scared/busy/unwell/lazy/sleepy] that make perfect sense.

So don't let it!

Otherwise we put it off… and we put it off… and we put it off… and opportunities pass us by. We watch our lives happen to us, rather than making stuff happen *for* us.

Startijen is intrinsic, which means the best place to look is *inside* your-self. The 5-second rule is an accelerator, but it also works as a hand-brake. An oft-obscured facet of personal improvement is that to be a better you, yes, you have to learn some new habits, but you also have to stop doing bad habits.

Feel like lighting a cigarette? 5, 4, 3, 2, 1… *nope*. I'm going to make a brew instead.

About to open a packet of biscuits and scoff the lot? *5, 4, 3, 2, 1 ... nope*. I reach for a piece of fruit instead.

Listening to your work colleague droning on and on about negative stuff and about to do the lazy thing and agree? *5, 4, 3, 2, 1 ... nope*. 'I get what you mean but have you thought about it like this...?'

Been in the gym for 20 minutes and feeling like you're not really in the mood? About to quit. 5, 4, 3, 2, 1 ... choose a new piece of equipment, schedule another 30 minutes and get cracking.

The Bretons must be glowing with pride. Yes, their language is under threat but if it disappears I do solemnly swear to keep *startijen* alive and kicking. The 5-second rule is *startijen* at its best. It's simple. It's free. It's quick. Best of all, the 5-second rule puts YOU in the driver's seat of your own life.

Finnish Strong

Next, let's go north. Think of all the places Santa could live and yet he chooses to have a place in Lapland. That takes me to Finland, currently sitting at #1 in the international league tables of happiness. There must be something we can learn from the Finns?

For a start they have *hyppytyynytyydytys*, a vowelless mouthful which translates as 'bouncy cushion satisfaction'. Imagine having an actual word for the feeling of plonking your backside onto your favourite cushion? No wonder they're so happy!

But Finnish culture runs deep. Here's a biggy...

As a lover of language, I find myself cringing when footballers massacre it. 'Sick as a parrot' and 'over the moon' still get an airing, but the biggest teeth grinder used to be when the player explained that he'd given 110%. Or occasionally 120%. An *X-Factor* contestant once vowed to give it 210% (random?) and I recall a Newcastle United footballer getting totally mixed up and suggesting the team had performed 360% better.

On reflection, that might be genius?

Anyhow, my teeth were wearing away because I'm an academic pedant. You can't give more than 100%. Basically, if you give a task *everything you've got*, that's 100% you've given. A hundred percent is your absolute maximum.

That is until I learned about the Finnish concept of *sisu* (pronounced 'SEE-su'), a small word that packs an enormous punch. *Sisu* relates to the psychological strength that allows a person to overcome extraordinary challenges. When you're running on empty and you're not sure you can carry on, *sisu* is your emergency 'reserve tank' that somehow keeps you going. It has no direct English translation. The closest I can give you is grit, bravery and resilience.

Footballers, I salute you. If humble pie had calories I'd be morbidly obese. You can give 110% if you end up giving *more* than you thought you had. It's a matter of mindset. *Sisu* is potent. It helps people exceed their known capabilities.

It's about the fundamental understanding that the best helping hands are at the end of your own arms. *Sisu* helps YOU help YOU when YOU need help the most. It's about digging in.

It's more than a word. *Sisu* encapsulates an entire philosophy. The first Finns settling in America in the 1870s gained a reputation as doggedly hard workers. They built tight-knit communities and helped each other out in lean times. Embedded in *sisu* is the fundamental truth that life is punctuated by major challenges. *Sisu* is about embracing these times and daring to greet misfortune like an old friend. It helps you greet challenges with a warm embrace. Have a chin wag with adversity. Reflect on times past when you had to get through similar tough times.

Thank the tough times for making you stronger.

Sisu is a steely determination to roll up your sleeves and crack on.

Best of all, it's about building character. We've somehow found ourselves in a vapid Kardashian culture where there's an emphasis on projecting an idealised version of life. Social media gives everyone a voice. Soapbox shops must be doing a roaring trade as we all clamour to be heard. *Sisu* has substance. It eschews the superficial and embraces the real. Large chunks of this book are underpinned by *sisu*.

Genuine success, the real you, going about your life without making a song and dance. *Sisu* – if you could bottle it, it'd be the elixir of *real* life. Other countries have sister concepts. *Ao nenna* (Icelandic) is the state of being bothered to do something. It's literally the ability and willingness to persevere through tasks that are hard or boring. After enduring tough times the Chinese have a wonderful recovery word – *kŭ qù gān lái* – literally 'from pain to sweetness'. It's the sense of happiness or relief after going through trying times.

We've all been there, done that. The difference is now you know what it's called!

Words That Have Stopped Me in My Tracks

'One way to get high blood pressure is to go mountain climbing over molehills.'
[Earl Wilson]

The sheer linguistic beauty of the Bakweri people of Cameroon can be heard with *womba*, the smile of a sleeping child.

The moon's reflection on water has a distinct word in Turkish – *yakamoz* – yet takes on an added feature in the Swedish *mångata*, literally, 'moon road' – the shimmering reflection that appears when the moon shines on the water.

In Greek there is one word, *psithirisma*, for the sound of wind whispering through the leaves of trees.

Now park the poetry. We're going deep…

Here's a concept that has had a profound impact on me. All the way from Japan I bring you the sublime beauty of *ichi-go ichi-e*, literally translated as, 'for this time only' and also as 'in this moment, an opportunity'. Originating from 16th-century tea ceremonies, *ichi-go ichi-e* recognises that everything we experience is a unique treasure that will never be repeated in the same way again. So, for example, on the surface, a cup of tea with your family might seem like an everyday occasion but each gathering is a unique experience. The exact same people having a cup of tea tomorrow will create a different atmosphere.

That means family set pieces that happen every day are *all* special. Each gathering is unique. So if we let them slip away without enjoying them, the moment will be lost forever.

It's had a profound effect on me. Becoming aware of *ichi-go ichi-e* helps me take my foot off the accelerator and remember that each morning I spend in the world, every moment I spend with my wife and children is infinitely valuable and deserves my full attention.

Don't postpone special moments. Each opportunity presents itself only once. If you don't embrace it, it's lost forever. It really is a case of life being now or never.

I've regressed to be a hunter–gatherer – not of wild pigs and berries, but of moments. *This* breakfast, *this* bedtime story, *this* walk, *this* trip to the supermarket, *this* time the cat sits on my knee, *this* frosty morning, *this* hug. Awareness of *ichi-go ichi-e* means I feel much less weighed down by the past or anxious about the future. It's a super-clever form of mindfulness that leaves you smiling inside.

The Danes have a more well-known, dare I say 'fashionable' equivalent: *hygge* (pronounced 'hoo-gah') – which brings them a lot of happiness. It hasn't got a direct English translation. The closest I can get is 'comfort', or 'cosy' or 'all snuggly and loved up'. It's a wonderful brand of happiness that's often associated with family time. Kind of like when it's a lazy Sunday morning and you're cuddled up on the sofa with your cat, watching cartoons, dressed in your onesie (you, not the cat).

It got me thinking that if it's good enough for the happiest people in the world, it's good enough for me. So I started looking out for *hygge* moments and, oh my goodness, I started spotting them everywhere. Coming inside on a cold winter's morning to a steaming mug of hot chocolate – that's definitely *hygge*. Family get-togethers at my mum's house, picking wild blackberries in the autumn, the smell of baking, seeing my breath on a cold morning, bonfire night, a yummy Sunday dinner, that first spoonful of Rice Krispies, lemon curd on toast, breaking the ice on a puddle, twinkly Christmas lights, the smell of rain on a hot pavement... they're all *hygge* too. For me, that is. Your *hygge* moments will be different.

And get this. I discovered that you don't need to have any money to find *hygge*. In fact, quite the opposite. Cheaper things are more hoo-gary than expensive ones. Eating home-made cake makes me happier than eating a bought cake. Drinking tea from my battered old mug gives me more happiness than sipping it from a posh china cup. A family lunch at my mum's gave me far more happiness than a fancy-pants restaurant. A board game is more *hygge* than a computer game. Slobbing around in my scruffy jeans and fave t-shirt makes me happier than getting dressed in an expensive suit and tie. A blustery day out at a British seaside resort is way more *hygge* than at an 85-degree Spanish one.

I delved a bit deeper into *hygge* and discovered that it's an entire attitude to life. Having a relaxed, cosy time with friends and family, often with coffee and cake, is good for the soul. In actual fact, the family and friends bit of that sentence is more important than the coffee and cake bit because it hints at what you already know – that relationships are crucial to happiness. Eating cake on your own might be very tasty but it's certainly not *hygge*.

Sharing cake with family or friends, that's more like it!

That's why having friends on social media is fine and dandy, but spending time with real flesh and blood chums, that's *hygge*.

I've found it hugely beneficial to my wellbeing, so here's some *hygge* homework. It changes as the seasons change. Spend a few minutes going through the seasons and listing what your *hygge* moments are. Don't overthink it. Remember, it's cosy, snuggly time when your inner glow shows up on the outside.

List your top 5 *hygge* moments for each season:

Spring

Summer

Autumn

Winter

And finally, Archimedes had his eureka moment in the bath. He was so excited about his water displacement realisation that, legend has it, he forgot to get dressed and ran down the street naked. Hey, I've had some exciting break-throughs in my life but have always managed to get my dressing gown on before I tell the world.

But if you look at some of the greatest thinkers, a pattern begins to emerge. Idling. Stillness. Boredom even.

Isaac Newton had his Aha! moment while sitting under an apple tree. He was in contemplative mood when an apple fell and, hey presto, gravity was invented. Carlo Rovelli writes that many of Einstein's greatest ideas came from when he '…spent a year loafing aimlessly'.[2] It seems you don't get anywhere by *not* wasting time.

Idleness, quiet time, sloth, boredom – whatever we choose to call it – is not an indulgence or a vice, it is as indispensable to the brain as vitamins are to the body.

But in a frantic world, boredom has been crowded out. It's not even a luxury. It's not viewed as something you can look forward to or deliberately create time for. It's seen as a vice. Something to be avoided. And yet the space and quiet that idleness provides is a necessary condition for standing back from life and seeing it whole, for making unexpected connections and waiting for the lightning strikes of inspiration.

> **Have you ever noticed that all your best ideas come when you're in the shower or out on a walk?**

Somewhat paradoxically, it seems that idleness and boredom might be necessary to getting your best work done. Hence I bring you *dolce far niente*, which kick-started my idleness in 2019. The Italian concept of 'the beauty of doing nothing without feeling guilty about it' was already a revelation and then along came COVID-19. The pandemic brought death and disruption, but also a sense of connection with those closest to me. An enforced time out, confined to quarters for 12 months, I committed to reading an hour a day. I also added a daily two-hour brisk walk and healthy food to my routine.

---

[2] Rovelli, C. (2015) *'What is time? What is space?* Rome, Italy: Di Renzo Editore.

My training business was in dire financial straits, and yet I was loving life. We were lucky. We had enough in the bank to sustain us for the foreseeable so I promised myself that when business rebounded, I would stay committed to doing less. COVID-19 was a speed bump in my life. I renewed my vows to being fully alive: for richer or poorer, in sickness and in health, till death I do depart, I will choose time over money.

It was, and still is, a case of financially poorer not richer. But *dolce far niente* has taught me to slow down without feeling guilty. The best investment of my limited time on earth is to spend it with people I love. Pre-pandemic I already knew that, but knowing and doing are not the same thing.

Of course, I could be wrong. I suppose it's just about feasible that I'll lie on my deathbed regretting that I didn't put more hours in at the office. But it's far more likely that I'll really wish I could have one more beer with my son Ollie, another long walk with my wife Lou, and one last good belly laugh with my daughter Sophie.

Life is too short to be busy.

Remember That Words Can Change Worlds

Manifesto reminder

1 Borrow the word *startijen* from the Bretons. Use the 5-second rule to kickstart your day.

2 Running on empty? Steal some *sisu* from the Finns. It's about tapping into your reserve tank.

3 Living too fast? Try *ichi-go ichi-e* from Japan. If everything is *one time only* it makes sense to slow down and experience as many moments as possible.

4 Those pesky Danes have known about *hygge* for centuries. I say keep your bacon, Carlsberg and LEGO. I'm importing hygge into my life.

5 *Dolce far niente* – guilt-free nothingness, all the way from Italy. I'm gradually getting better at doing nothing but not sure I'll ever be able to fully drop the guilt. Best of luck with it.

Trivial Pursuit.

[Advance warning: pledges 8 and 9 are besties. Inseparable. Please concentrate while reading pledge 8 because we'll be testing you on it in 9. Thank you.]

1987 was a significant year for me. Within 12 months of us meeting, Helen, my then girlfriend, decided that despite my love of football, my complete ineptitude at DIY, and that I was missing both nails on my big toes (apologies for the detail but it's important), spending the rest of her life with me seemed like a good idea.

As I write this we've been married 33 years. My love of football has never diminished, my toenails never grew back, and I remain 'DIY intolerant'.

1987 was also the year that I went to see U2. Classic when-they-were-good U2. Bono and the gang were in their *Joshua Tree* phase. In May that year they released the enduring anthem 'I Still Haven't Found What I'm Looking For'.

Much less so nowadays, but for half a century I was Bono-esque. There was definitely something missing but I could never quite put my finger on what that 'certain something' was.

As a youngster I dreamed of one day being famous. The only modicum of skill I possessed was in acting, and I thought a career as an actor would pave the way not only to fame and recognition but also to a permanent state of happiness. Looking back, working as a bank clerk in Chorlton-cum-Hardy certainly didn't seem the most obvious route to achieving fame and fortune as an actor. I opened a lot of current accounts but never to an opening night of adoring theatre goers.

My search for happiness continued, always with a common thread. The desire to find happiness in an event, a person, or an achievement continued to grow. My daily mantra could be summed up as *'I'll be happy when...'*

The nagging discontent I felt was undoubtedly fuelled by the Hollywood films I saw as a child, and I lived life constantly pursuing the pot of gold at the end of the rainbow. I genuinely believed that when I'd found my gold my problems would disappear and I would finally feel satisfied that my life had meaning and purpose.

However, after years of soul searching I've come to the stark realisation that it wasn't fame I was after. It wasn't money. It wasn't even happiness.

What I longed for deep in my innermost being was to feel loved. To feel I belonged, and that despite my countless flaws, failures and lack of toenails, I was still lovable and accepted by others.

You see, I've slowly recognised that the trap I had become ensnared in was seeking an external solution to an internal problem.

And – at the risk of sounding cliché – I was looking for the keys to my happiness in someone else's pocket. I believed happiness was a destination – Happiness Central – a place you get to arrive at…eventually. It would be worth the sacrifice, the struggle, the stress, because once I was 'there', I'd step onto the platform at HC and be able to send Bono a text: 'Mate, you know that thing you've been looking for. I've only gone and found it!'

I don't blame myself for buying into this myth.

The nightly news is not filled with analysis of how happy the citizens are. Most governments' adopted measurement of 'success' is how fast the economy grows. If it fails to add 2 or 3 percentage points every year, the news kicks up a fuss and voters abandon ship. The end result is that we live in a society where there is always going to be someone trying to sell you something.

Fact: if everyone was happy with their life, car, clothes, watch, partner, weight, mobile phone contract, body shape, energy levels, shoes, breakfast cereal and motor insurance…the economy would grind to a halt. Capitalism is perpetuated by constantly agitating us with dis-satisfaction. The job of the marketeers is to manufacture desire. Once they've created a burning yearning, the actual manufacturers swing into action.

> **Materialism puts you firmly into the relentless pursuit of more. It's like fighting the Hydra. Lop off a head and more serpents spring up.**

Of course, chasing more is wrapped up with the notion of bettering ourselves. Maybe this constant need to find happiness is what drives progress and our desire for achievement. Perhaps such an outlook is not all bad – it has its upsides.

Adopting such an outlook has developed within me a desire to achieve, to seize the day and not waste my life. The search has given me the energy and determination to build a business from ground zero, it's been the catalyst to me writing books and to wanting to make a difference. And I genuinely believe that a degree of mild dissatisfaction is good. It woos us to want more, never to be completely satisfied – to want to make progress.

And that's a good thing.

But it leads me onto a very big series of questions. Have we been looking for happiness in the wrong place? Have we been searching for happiness – or what we think will make us happy – found it, and then felt let down?

> **Have we found our version of fame, fortune, recognition and achievement – and yet still not felt satisfied?**

Indeed, here's the big one that began to reframe my thinking: *could you be happier even if nothing in the world around you changed?*

It's a perfectly simple question that took me to a hitherto unexplored depth of understanding. Let the question roll around your mind a couple of times. *Could you be happier even if nothing in the world around you changed?*

My answer, to me, was 'yes'. Which was a bit of a shock. 'Yes' was an admission that I could be happier. The world didn't need to change; in fact the world wasn't going to change to accommodate my happiness demands. The world was going to continue to do what the world does. I had the potential to be happier, yet I wasn't being. The penny-dropping moment was the realisation that the biggest thing stopping me being happy was me.

So instead of trying to fix the world (to be fair, the effort was exhausting me), I turned my attention inwards. If I could somehow fix me, maybe the world would seem more accommodating.

So I began to engage with me. The personal upgrade from me 1.0 to me 2.0 resulted in the flood gates opening, first with a trickle, then with a gush. I learned that happiness is about engaging with and experiencing life in all its fullness. In its highs and its lows, in its joys and its tears. It's about participating in life and discovering meaning and purpose.

This next point is so crucial.

Happiness is a by-product of living life well.

I quit making it a goal.

To be clear, I'm not suggesting we dump our dreams and desires. Goals are good. Challenging yourself to get better is healthy. Seeking ways to improve society is important. And will you be happy achieving success? Of course you will.

But just remember, happiness is dynamic, not static. It doesn't have to be on hold until you've achieved your intended aim. Aspects of happiness such as contentment and inner peace can be experienced every day, whatever you're facing. Feelings fade and fluctuate. Emotions come and go. But inner happiness can remain because it's not based solely on external factors, but on your own inner sense of wellbeing. It's experienced sometimes not because of what is going on around you, but despite what's going on.

> **Let's pursue opportunities and let's promote gratitude and kindness, but let's park the actual pursuit of happiness.**

Let's enjoy it whilst we're caught up living life well, rather than holding it hostage until some arbitrary event occurs and we feel we can now give ourselves permission to snuggle into it.

Here's the deal. When it comes to happiness, you don't have to find it, chasing it is futile, you can't choose it and you don't have to earn it – you simply have to learn to open up to it.

The Contents of Contentment

In a weird re-working of traditional thinking I'd like you to get your head around what, for me, is probably the most impactful sentence in the entire book. In order to open the happiness flood gates you have to turn conventional wisdom on its head. Here's how it really works:

Once you're content, you have enough.

On first reading it'll seem backwards. Why? Because you'll have fallen into the trap of thinking that once you have enough, you'll be content. Today's world makes us feel like we are not enough because we don't *have* enough. If you haven't got a smart phone, you want one. If you've got one, you want a smarter one. If yours is already super smart you want a nicer phone case.

So you buy whatever product it happens to be and, guess what, you do feel happy and shiny. Sometimes for a whole hour! And then there's another advert with another shiny happy person, even shinier and happier than the previous one, and she's got a different product. That must be what you need. Some people chase 'more stuff' for their entire lives. Which makes perfect sense as long as you think that having more stuff makes you happy.

Unless you learn to break free.

Here's an advert you'll never see. Imagine a normal person. Let's use YOU as the example. Imagine that you switch on the TV and you are in the advert. You'd be like, okay, that's weird. The camera is pointed at you. Just you. No airbrushed perfection. It's you wearing your Monday face. Hair's fine, if a little squiffy. There's a bit of dried-up breakfast cereal stuck on your upper lip. Your eyebrows need plucking, and there are a couple of nose hairs that could do with some attention. You're wearing your jimjams and there's a bit of sleep on the corner of your right eye.

The camera is fixated on you, and the voiceover begins...

'Know what? You're perfectly fine as you are. For a start, you smell pretty good. Most of your clothes are actually quite cool. In fact you look super-amazing in that really old jumper that's lost its shape. You know the one. The jumper your gran knitted for you last Christmas. Your hair is nice and your skin is lovely. Your car's not the latest, but it's fine. It gets you from A to B in comfort and it's got four coffee cup holders and a secret sunglasses compartment. I mean, that's pretty cool. That phone of yours isn't the latest or smartest, but it's perfectly fine. Tell you what, why not keep it? You've got plenty of decent trainers, scarves and hats. You can cook a half-decent meal so you don't need pizza Deliverood to your door. Ditto exceedingly good cakes – sure you can buy one from the supermarket, but a homemade one is better. Feel free to crack on with your life because you most definitely don't need what we're selling.'

The reason you've never seen an advert like that is because whoever wrote it would be sacked. For telling you the actual truth! Every single ad on the TV, in a mag, online or on a billboard is designed to make you unhappy with your life as it currently is. And we know this, right? We know that we're constantly being sold to.

I tune in to watch my football team on TV and am slack jawed to discover that the substitutions are sponsored by the local Toyota car dealership and the number of minutes of added time are brought to me by a company that sells pine furniture.

To be clear, I'm absolutely not suggesting that buying stuff is a bad thing. But there is something wrong with the bonkers rate at which we've been consuming products. This planet of ours… Mother Earth… she's wheezing a bit. The forests are being cleared, orangutans re-homed and the oceans polluted so we can produce more stuff to buy/eat/wear.

It's important to understand that if there's something missing in your life, it's most probably YOU. Therefore a nuanced but important point is centred on 'enoughness'.

> **To switch off your want-ometer you need to learn to be satisfied with what you already have rather than lusting after what you haven't.**

I have to say, it's a pretty cool happiness hack. The world is a bit like an all-you-can-eat buffet, with everything spread out before you. Contentment is less about knowing where to start, and more about knowing when to stop.

Envy, Gluttony, Greed, Lust, Pride, Sloth, and Wrath

Of the seven deadly sins only envy is no fun at all. The problem is that an envy industry has grown up, with outrage factories belching out toxic bad news and social comparison fumes that are inhaled by us all.

It's damaging. In really bad cases, the envy industry shows up in depression, anxiety and needless worry. One of the ailments of the envy industry is 'comparisonitis', a nasty little affliction that causes a rash of jealousy. You'll know if you've got it – your eyes develop a tinge of green. Other symptoms include a sense of restlessness and a bad case of wanting stuff. Lots of stuff. The latest and shiniest stuff. You end up lusting after other people's houses, cars, holidays, jobs, kids…

Wishing you were living someone else's life is, in most instances, just a little bit sad. It means you've not truly woken up to the magnificence of the life you're actually living.

Good news. There is a cure, an oh-so-simple remedy that will rid you of the milder form of comparisonitis. This two-step medicine will shift the feeling in a couple of weeks.

Step one: you need to write a list of 30 things that you really appreciate but take for granted. Phrased differently, what have you got to be thankful for? Or, differently again, what 30 things/people are you lucky to have in your life but might have taken your eye off?

Anything goes. Mine would include clean drinking water, oranges, trees, vegetable samosas, warm showers, memories, pencil sharpeners, being British, Toy Story 2, lamp posts, music, the smell of autumn, oxygen, white blood cells, Hans Zimmer, homemade jam and walls with moss on.

Step one of the cure for comparisonitis is to write your list and marvel at what you already have in your life. This basically makes your envy less green. We promise you, most people spend a massive amount of their time grumbling about what they *haven't* got whereas your list of 30 should prod you in the other direction. Go through your list one by one, allowing yourself a few seconds to focus on each item. Linger just long enough so the feeling of gratitude squirms right down into your stomach.

Please note, this activity is borrowed from actual therapy. It's tried and tested. Thinking about what you're grateful for each day and taking the time to write those things down is the best homework ever because it gives headspace to each one. It means the great things in your life won't just pass you by anymore. You'll notice them. And you'll realise that, even if you've had the toughest of days, you've actually got a fair amount of good stuff and nice people in your life.

As you keep practising, you'll learn more about what brings you joy, so you can start focusing your time and energy on the things that make you the happiest/best version of yourself.

Step two of our comparisonitis cure is to switch your focus. Instead of trying to match up against everyone else, start matching up to your best self. Comparing yourself with yourself is where the magic sauce really is. So instead of comparing yourself with the other runners and riders, you get to ask a much better question: *Am I a slightly better person than I was yesterday?*

If you can answer 'yes' to that on a regular basis, you'll be growing. Keep at it, daily. As your confidence and self-esteem blossom, your comparisonitis will melt away.

We'll finish this section with a passage that is almost certainly fake news. It's based on the words of Steve Gouves who, rather sadly, died of pancreatic cancer, age 56, leaving a $7 billion fortune. But your sadness will be lessened if we tell you that 'Steve' was most probably created to make a point so what follows might not be strictly true, but we're including it because its meaning is strong.

Here's fake Steve's famous fake last words…

'In other eyes, my life is the essence of success, but aside from work, I have a little joy, and in the end wealth is just a fact of life to which I am accustomed. At this moment, lying on the bed, sick and remembering all my life, I realize that all my recognition and wealth that I have is meaningless in the face of imminent death.

'You can hire someone to drive a car for you, make money for you – but you cannot rent someone to carry the disease for you. One can find material things, but there is one thing that cannot be found when it is lost – "life".

'Treat yourself well, and cherish others. As we get older we are smarter, and we slowly realize that the watch is worth $30 or $300 – both of which show the same time. Whether we carry a purse worth $30 or $300 – the amount of money in the wallets are the same. Whether we drive a car worth $150,000, or a car worth $30,000 – the road and distance are the same, we reach the same destination… If the house we live in is 300 square meters, or 3000 square meters – the loneliness is the same.

'Your true inner happiness does not come from the material things of this world. Whether you're flying first class, or economy class – if the plane crashes, you crash with it. So, I hope you understand that when you have friends or someone to talk to – this is true happiness!'

Steve stated what he called his Five Undeniable Facts:

1 Do not educate your children to be rich. Educate them to be happy, so when they grow up they will know the value of things, not the price.

2 Eat your food as medicine, otherwise you will need to eat your medicine as food.

3 Whoever loves you will never leave you, even if he has 100 reasons to give up. He will always find one reason to hold on.

4 There is a big difference between being human and human being.

5 If you want to go fast – go alone! But if you want to go far – go together!

And, according to Steve, the six best doctors in the world are:

1 Sunlight
2 Rest
3 Exercise
4 Diet
5 Self-confidence
6 Friends

Fake news at its most poignant.

Fake Amen x

Call Off the Search

Manifesto reminder

1 The last I heard Bono *still* hadn't found what he was looking for. Maybe he's looking in the wrong place?

2 Happiness is not something to strive for. It's a by-product of living life well.

3 Happiness isn't something you can choose but it is something that you can open up to. It's about allowing it in.

4 Once you're content, you have enough.

5 The materialism treadmill is like a real treadmill: it's exhausting and goes nowhere.

6 Comparisonitis is a deadly disease. It makes you green around the gills. Our two-step remedy is:

   a Focus on what you have got rather than lusting after what you haven't.

   b Compare you against you. Small improvements every day means you're moving in the right direction.

7 Those fake doctors in that fake news report about fake 'Steve'... they're worth consulting.

Memento Mori

My grandma used to talk to herself, out loud. There was a running commentary – her to her – as she went about her day. It was nearly always negative.

'Oh my goodness, Eileen. Why on earth did you leave the soup boiling for so long? It's ruined. What on earth will people think?...'

'Why on earth did I peg my washing out? I knew it would rain.'

'Heaven's above, Eileen, you'd forget your own head if it wasn't screwed on…'

It was really weird, especially because her name was Margaret.

My grandma had a glass cabinet in her kitchen. On the first three shelves were the everyday cups, saucers, plates, salt pot, milk jug and suchlike. It was a hotchpotch of different items from different eras. Nothing matched. Lots of it was chipped. I'd describe it as 'rustic' and 'homely'.

The top shelf was reserved for her best Royal Crown Derby china cups, saucers and plates. This was the pristine shelf where everything matched and nothing was chipped. It was special and more or less untouchable.

My gran used the top shelf for top-notch visitors. We had an architect around one time. I remember him qualifying for the top shelf. I think the vicar got his tea in Crown Derby but, day to day, we ate and guzzled from the bottom shelf.

Please note, this is not a grumble. None of this crossed my mind when I was growing up. It's just the way things were. In fact, it made perfect sense to save the best china for special occasions. We all do it. It's not just cups and saucers. The philosophy is neatly encapsulated in the term 'Sunday best': special clothes for church, expensive perfume for a night out, best Champagne for something worth celebrating and sexiest knickers for date night.

Plot spoiler alert: pledge #9 is about NOT doing that.

But in order to explain, I'm going to have to make you uncomfortable. That's why we've snuck this manifesto pledge in towards the end. We figure if you've got this far, you'll be expecting – maybe even welcoming – a sucker punch.

In which case I'm about to drag you down the darkened back alley of wellbeing and beat seven bells of happiness into you. In the dark recesses of our mind lies the Latin phrase, memento mori, 'remember death'. It tallies with the more modern Terror Management Theory. The clue's in the name folks. It's hilariously un-funny.

Death, and in particular the awareness of it, is something that's most probably unique to the human species. I say 'probably' because it's unprovable. Small-brained animals almost certainly don't contemplate the prospect of not being here. Your cat, for example. She doesn't fret about getting cancer or whether she's used eight of her lives so be careful because the next one is curtains.

Large-brained animals... who knows? Elephants have long memories. They can recall the death of loved ones but that doesn't necessarily equate to worrying about it. Humans, however – we have an in-built death awareness radar, a sense of scarcity, as time ticks away. There's a lingering sense that the clocks are watching you, their ticking counting down your heartbeats.

The scary thing about death is not the dying bit itself. Admittedly, that bit doesn't hold the prospect of being a great deal of fun, but my view is that everyone in the history of human beings has died, or will die, so it's a racing certainty that I will too. You might need to sit down for this next bit, but your life will also come to an end.

The 'terror' bit isn't the pain or the last breath or having drips in your arm or an oxygen tube up your nose. Rather, the spine chiller is when you get towards the final stages and realise there are boxes unticked. Big ones. Like cycling in Patagonia.

To use the earlier example, your small-brained cat isn't fretting about leaving that one off her bucket list. Neither, I would imagine, is the large-brained elephant. But here's where the capacity for human angst ratchets to uncomfortable levels – we eventually come to realise (often a few decades too late) that it's not the BIG unticked boxes that matter. Sure, it's unfortunate that I never got around to booking my flight to Buenos Aries, but as the fat lady of death is clearing her throat, it's the small unticked boxes that really count.

The walks I didn't take because it was drizzling. Or it wasn't actually drizzling but the sky was looking a bit grey so it might drizzle. The hugs I didn't have. The picnics I was too busy for. The puddles I didn't splash in. The rainbows I missed. The night sky I failed to look up at. The dances I didn't dance and the roller coasters I didn't roll or coast.

In the science of wellbeing, it's the sum of these little things that add up to being a big thing called 'happiness'.

> **Essentially, the things you do every day are more important than the things you do once in a while.**

Back to the dark alley. Most people hide the prospect of death away in the back of their mind, but we're all one doctor's visit away from it becoming THE all-consuming thing. Either a rude reminder of your own mortality, or the death of someone you love. All of a sudden, not dying emerges from the darkest recesses of your awareness and shoulder barges its way to centre stage. *Not dying* becomes the #1 goal.

These cataclysmic events cause the penny to drop. We realise that we spend almost all of eternity not being alive. In the history of the universe, we occupy such a brief flicker of time, and if life is such a wonderful and precious gift, it'd be a terrible shame to send it back unopened.

Quite often these earth-shattering instances also bring about a shift in emphasis and happiness begins to reveal itself in all its wondrous simplicity. The moments of pure joy are brought from behind the magic curtain.

The big reveal?

It's all been a sleight of mind. Happiness has been hidden in plain sight.

Yes, the whole damn time! While you've been madly pursing it at the weekend, or on holiday or next year or when you retire, happiness has been waiting patiently for you to discover it, right under your nose.

I know, you could kick yourself for being fooled by something so simple!

Let me turn the warm-heartedness into a deadly chill, via a true story that also acts as an example. I know a 30-year-old man whose wife was diagnosed with something utterly woeful that shrunk her horizons from 60 more years to just a few weeks. That's an unimaginably cruel scenario. (I have tears as I type these words.) Roy visited his wife in hospital, bringing flowers, like you absolutely would. Marie spent a whole hour with the flowers. She smelled them, touched them, looked at them... and then smelled, touched and looked again. And again.

Why?

Because these might be the last flowers she ever experiences.

For me, it boils down to this.

Remember from earlier, we suggested that happiness isn't something you can choose, but it absolutely is something you can allow in. So it's time to open the door. `Hello happiness, you gorgeous thing! How rude of me. I actually didn't hear you knocking! How long have you been waiting outside? All eternity? Gosh, sorry about that. Come on in and I'll put the kettle on. I don't suppose you've tried Bono's door? Apparently he's been looking for you too.'

In the interests of coming absolutely clean, my co-author and I are great believers in life *before* death. Bottom line? Life is time.

To be precise, time is all we ever have.

To be precisely precise, NOW is all you ever have.

Busy, Busy, Busy, Busy, Busy, Busy, Busy. . . *Dead!*

The paradox of time: The faster you race, the further you are from the present moment.

Our revelation that NOW is all you ever have is hardly new. Confucius was big on the present moment. Buddhists call it *upekkha*, Muslims *aslama*, Jews *hishtavut*, Greeks *authymia*, and the Stoics have *apatheia*. They're all subtle variations on the theme of being present in every heartbeat.

When all the guidebooks tell you to eat in the same restaurant, you eat in THAT restaurant. And when all the wisdom of the ancient world has come to the same conclusion it pays to book a seat at THAT philosophical table.

In English it might be best described as stillness or inner peace, aka 'mindfulness'.

To be honest, despite the apparent simplicity of the concept, I struggled with NOW for years (that's a weird sentence). I had trouble tuning into the wavelength of the present moment before realising the really good news: NOW gives you lots of chances to catch on. The nice thing about the present is that it's always here. It's hangs around for all eternity. It keeps showing up to give you a second, third, fourth... *billionth* chance.

Remember, some people will go their entire life living anywhere other than in this present moment. Life can send you a wake-up call and when the health alarm goes off, people realise they've wasted a lot of time while life was 'normal'. It's not just what they did with their time (working, checking emails, scrolling, tutting, commuting, grumbling, worrying...), the regrets will almost certainly come from realising they cared about the wrong things.

That sentence has huge philosophical tonnage so let me unpick it...

For too many people, year after year, their attention was somewhere else. Somewhere other than now. There will come a day when you'll look back and realise that your attention was snagged by utter nonsense. In fact, I think 'hijacked' might be a better word? Watching a bad movie for the sixth time, losing hours of your precious life on social media, bickering with someone you love, chuntering about your job, regretting your past, worrying about your future, grumbling about your commute, getting upset about tomorrow's weather forecast, snared by clickbait, comparing your humdrum life with someone's Facebook showreel, being too busy to notice the flowers...

> **The alternative to chasing happiness is to pause and give happiness a chance to catch up with you.**

The liberating truth that opens the door to happiness is that it starts and ends with a shift of thinking. A shift away from manipulating your thoughts towards the insight that you are the thinker.

Remember, I led you down a dark alley where I was gonna beat some happiness into you, so here's the solar plexus punch: the past is a memory. It's a thought arising in the present. The future is anticipation, which is another thought, rising in the now. Those thoughts come with complications. Each thought comes armed with an emotion. Some thoughts bring lovely emotions but all too often they come armed with something that stings. Some thoughts are nuclear. They can detonate anger, self-loathing, jealousy and envy. In some cases, our thinking is killing us. Literally.

So far I've led you down this dark alley to reveal that all we truly ever have is *this* moment.

If you dare to take one step further it's this; *Gosh, this moment is busy!*

There are a million priorities, all shouting for your attention. Amidst the bedlam, it's easy for happiness to get crowded out. We often struggle to connect with the present moment because we're too busy chasing a better moment. A future moment. You give happiness a wave. *'Cooee, I can see you over there,'* you shout. *'Hang on, happiness, I'm coming to get you. I've just get to get these emails done and this work report written. I'll catch up with you on Saturday.'*

Indeed, let's take another step down the dark alley. If you're placing your happiness at the weekend, or when you get promoted, or married, or divorced, or on holiday (or anywhere other than right now), the present moment becomes an irritation. We get impatient, anxious or frustrated with the present moment. NOW becomes something to be rushed through. You're in a hurry to find happiness over there so you barge the present moment out of the way.

In a world riddled with anxiety, stress and panic, manifesto pledge #9 hints at a MASSIVE happiness truth. Quit comparing and call off the search. Now is all you ever have.

So it pays to treat the present moment with fewer sharp elbows and more of a warm embrace.

Sure, you can wait for the health scare to shake you into action. Loads of people do. Your trip to the doctor escalates into her suggesting you pop into hospital for some tests. Her smile is meant to be reassuring but it's just a little too strained. She has a worrying tone of voice as she makes the call. Worse still, she pulls in some favours to get you seen quickly.

Why such urgency?

Memento mori! Shit!

Oh, and one more thing before we move on. What most people don't realise is that feeling amazing right now, in this very moment, also affects your past and future. It's like putting on a pair of rose-tinted past and future specs. When you feel great in THIS moment, your past seems kind of okay too. All of a sudden those bad times don't seem so bad and you dealt with those challenges pretty well and those embarrassing moments were, in hindsight, really quite funny.

Happiness in this moment also means your future seems rather exciting and your ambitions are do-able. You stride purposefully towards a horizon lit by a red evening sky that shepherds would love.

The Upper Cut

I've heard life summarised as hatch, match and dispatch. Basically, the three records inked into the world database are your birth, marriage and death certificates.

Inevitably, that lump-in-the-throat moment came. My gran reached the 'dispatch' phase. With one of the most fabulous women in the world gone, the extended family and a bunch of hangers on did what you do. We trudged back from the church to Gran's house where there would be sandwiches, cakes and tea.

My Grandma would have been pleased to know that her death was deemed an occasion special enough for us all to be sipping PG Tips from her very best Crown Derby china collection.

Oh, the irony. The tea set she'd spent a lifetime *not* using was being filled and refilled at her own funeral. I reflected on my pristine cup, saucer and matching plate and couldn't help thinking, I wish they'd been chipped and cracked and used every single day.

Saving your best for a special occasion takes on a different meaning when you understand that life is the ultimate special occasion.

No, scrub that.

NOW is the ultimate special occasion.

Engage with the Only Moment in Time

Manifesto reminder

1 LIFE: sorry to be the bringer of bad news, but nobody gets out alive.

2 The worrying thing about death is not death itself. Getting to the end and realising you've not truly lived... that's terrifying!

3 After 4,000 years of trying, mindfulness has finally become fashionable in the west.

4 You are doomed to live forever in a place called NOW.

5 NOW gets crowded out. It's easy to rush through this moment to get to a new moment – a better one – somewhere over there... [Plot spoiler alert: there is no 'other moment'. Just this one.]

6 Therefore NOW is the ultimate special occasion.

Most people are familiar with the term déjà vu, a strange sensation that you've been here before. There's a little-known personal development equivalent: déjà moo, a sense of the same old bullshit being recycled. We're guessing that if you were feeling grumpy, you could accuse pledges 1–9 of being recycled. We sincerely hope not. But they could be contorted. That accusation *could* be made.

But not so for pledge 10.

[1] From an original idea from the tremendously creative Paul 'Wolfie' Field: https://www .artofbrilliance.co.uk/meet-the-team/paul-field/

To prepare you for the plot twists of life, we've designed our final pledge to be a challenge. Well, more of a question actually. In fact, it's not even a question, it's a game.

Get your imagination fired up because we want you to imagine you're representing your country in the Olympics. It's your imagination so you can pick any city you want: Rome, New York, Rio, Sydney, Barcelona, Coventry, Stockton on Tees. Literally anywhere. Next, picture the opening ceremony, with all the athletes entering the stadium, holding their national flag, waving to the adoring crowd.

So, yes, it's kind of like the normal Olympics, but with a difference.

Quite a big difference actually.

The normal Olympics take place every 4 years. It's an exotic gathering where the best in the world take on the best in the world. It's great entertainment because they're all so fast or bouncy or throwy or bendy or stretchy or balancey or swimmy or rowey or jumpy or strong. Ditto the Winter Olympics. Shooting headfirst down an icy hill on a baking tray – it's bonkers and brilliant at the same time.

The skill and talent on show is amazing. Which got us thinking, what if there was an Olympics for everyday things that require no skill or talent?

Absolutely none.

We're calling it the 'Everyday Olympics'. The clue's in the name. Rather than every 4 years, it happens *every single day* in an everyday town and it consists of ten events that we can all take part in.

It's a decathlon. Here are our ten everyday events that require zero skill or talent:

1. Working hard
2. Smiling
3. Having good manners
4. Being passionate about life
5. Expressing gratitude
6. Encouraging others
7. Having a positive attitude
8. Being super kind
9. Showing up on time
10. Looking after your physical health

Manifesto pledge 10 boils down to a simple question. Take another look into the mirror of personal responsibility and ask yourself – honestly – if you were competing in these ten everyday events, would you make the podium?

And with your hand on your heart, is there anything actually stopping you from going for gold?

From this day forth, I...

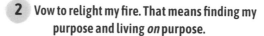

THE HAPPINESS REVOLUTION
YOUR 10 MANIFESTO PLEDGES

 1 Solemnly swear to be my own bestie. No more shame or guilt. I am flawed beauty and I'm happy with that.

2 Vow to relight my fire. That means finding my purpose and living *on* purpose.

 3 Pledge to take care of my physical self.

4 Commit to acknowledging life's small print. It's not, fair and I'm comfortable with that.

 5 Promise to value my values.

 6 Will dare to swap SMART objectives for Huge Unbelievably Great Goals.

7 Will live by some of those wonderful new words from around the world, especially *ichi-go ichi-e*, *hygge* and *dolce far niente*. I might even drop them into everyday conversation to impress my family and friends.

 8 Will call off the search. Happiness isn't something to it is chase but something I can open up to. I get that.

 9 Promise to fall in love with the only moment in time: *right now*.

10 Vow to represent my country at the Everyday Olympics. By default, that means I promise to get the everyday basics right.

Signature (ink, blood and tears are acceptable)

 SIGNED: _____   DATED: _____

Part 3

ALLEGORY

[al-uh-gawr-ee]

i A poem, play, picture, etc., in which the apparent meaning of the characters and events is used to symbolise a deeper moral or spiritual meaning

ii The technique or genre that this represents

iii Use of such symbolism to illustrate truth or a moral

197

Part 1 was our call to arms – sign up to a revolution of wellbeing and human flourishing. Be the firestarter, so to speak.

In Part 2 we laid out the joining conditions. The non-negotiables. The manifesto pledges. **YOUR** happiness pledges: 10 promises – you to you – that you do solemnly swear to build into your life. A reminder, these are they:

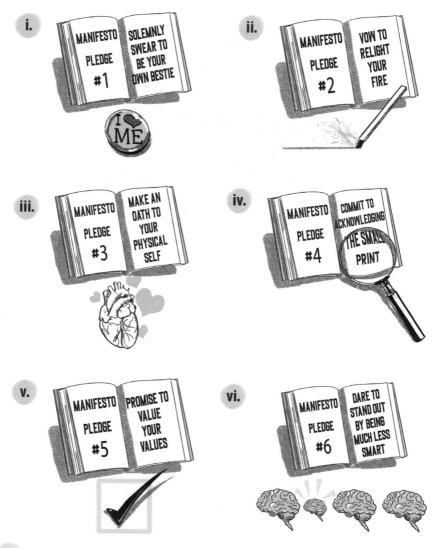

i. MANIFESTO PLEDGE #1 — SOLEMNLY SWEAR TO BE YOUR OWN BESTIE

ii. MANIFESTO PLEDGE #2 — VOW TO RELIGHT YOUR FIRE

iii. MANIFESTO PLEDGE #3 — MAKE AN OATH TO YOUR PHYSICAL SELF

iv. MANIFESTO PLEDGE #4 — COMMIT TO ACKNOWLEDGING THE SMALL PRINT

v. MANIFESTO PLEDGE #5 — PROMISE TO VALUE YOUR VALUES

vi. MANIFESTO PLEDGE #6 — DARE TO STAND OUT BY BEING MUCH LESS SMART

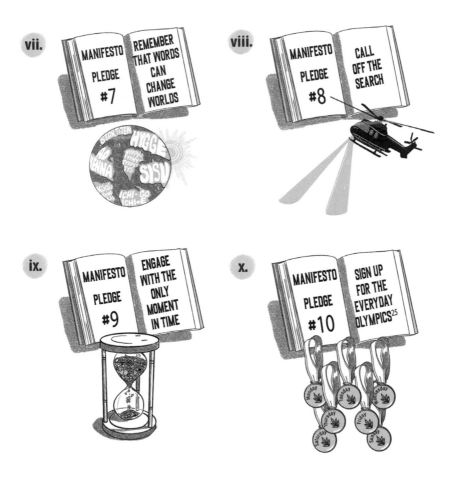

vii. MANIFESTO PLEDGE #7 — REMEMBER THAT WORDS CAN CHANGE WORLDS

viii. MANIFESTO PLEDGE #8 — CALL OFF THE SEARCH

ix. MANIFESTO PLEDGE #9 — ENGAGE WITH THE ONLY MOMENT IN TIME

x. MANIFESTO PLEDGE #10 — SIGN UP FOR THE EVERYDAY OLYMPICS[25]

Part 3 is a bonus section. At the outset, we explained that you'd bagged two authors for the price of one. Now we've only gone and upgraded you to 20% **EXTRA FREE!**

We figure that if you've got this far, you're on board. You're one of the smart ones, the interested few who not only buy books but actually read them too! That means you can work things out for yourself.

So here are some allegories according to the Prof and the Doc. The point about an allegory is that **NO EXPLANATIONS ARE PROVIDED**.

Thank you for getting this far. We are confident you'll find the not-so-hidden meanings.

LIFE LAG

It had been my most hectic working year ever. I'd been building a business, working stupid hours, chasing my dream, straining every nerve and sinew in the pursuit of 'success'.

I found myself in the bizarre situation of flying to Australia to do a keynote. As ridiculous as it sounds, I was destroying my marriage, my energy and the environment by undertaking a three-day round trip for a single hour of work. The plan was to land in Melbourne, do my thing, and fly back *the same night*.

I was exhausted before the Boeing's wheels even left Heathrow but forced myself to stay awake. Why? I had work to do. I spent the London to Singapore stretch totally absorbed in catching up with myself.

A 4-hour stopover at Changi Airport was another opportunity to work. Email connection secured, I knew there would be a deluge of messages as soon as I logged on.

I noticed a poster advertising a butterfly garden on the top floor of Singapore Airport. Yes, a butterfly garden. In an airport!

It sounded like a decent place to kill 4 hours so I paid a few dollars and gave it a go. 'Surreal' is an over-used word so I'm trying not to use it, but I'm guessing that if you look it up the definition could well be: *Changi Airport is the most modern of international airports and yet, somewhere on the top floor is a tranquil garden with fountains and butterflies.*

I found a park bench (I know, the phrase is jarring) and made myself comfy. It was the most un-airporty scene. I was sitting under a tree, listening to the waterfall and watching the butterflies. A short while later a bunch of school kids came in, a whole class of them, aged about 6, causing a disturbance of the peace. The children took one look at the butterflies and set about chasing them; jumping, running, whooping with glee. We're in an indoor bubble. It's tropical. The kids are soon drenched in sweat as they continue to leap and grab at the butterflies.

Except for one child. It took me a while to notice but one of the kids was standing in the corner of the atrium, stock still.

And this child was covered in butterflies.

Pause for Thought

Note, at the time I smiled and thought *'that's pretty cool'* before returning to my emails. I caught my flight, did my Australian talk and flew home as per the crazy schedule. I continued to work for the next 2 years with the same frenzy as previously. I was living in a state of close-to-but-not-quite exhaustion. I never gave the butterfly moment a second thought.

Then, in March 2020, along came a pandemic. It brought illness, death and social distancing. It was also my butterfly moment.

What's yours?

THE PARABLE OF COTTON CANDY

Everyone worries, but if there was an Olympics for worrying Candy's mum would be going for gold. In fact she was so good at worrying that she started to worry about her worrying. Then she started to get worried that she was worrying too much about worrying, which worried her some more.

Told you she was good!

Candy's mum lived with Candy's dad, in a house that they worried might be too small, in a neighbourhood that they worried might be too rough. Candy's dad was also a worrier, but in a slightly different way. He was what we might call an over-thinker. He specialised in imagining the worst, and if that happens it'd lead to something dire, and if that happened it'd trigger something completely terrible...

A sort of worst-case-scenario dominoes.

You get the picture.

A worrier and an over-thinker who sat and watched the news every night – war, famine, disasters, volcanoes, pandemics, dodgy politicians, job losses, forest fires, plane crashes, terrible weather, global warming, economic catastrophe – the world sure seemed like a terrible place.

Candy's mum and dad totally forgot that the news broadcasts all the worst disasters, wars and earthquakes from across the world. It slipped their mind that that's what 'news' is – deviations from the norm.

They had temporary amnesia that they lived in Sheffield which was safe and nice and non-quakey. It never crossed their minds that there hadn't been a plane crash in Sheffield since, well, forever. Famine-wise, the supermarket had once run out of brown sauce and Candy's dad reminded Candy's mum that there had been a war, back in the year 1455 - 'It were us against them Lancastrians' and 'if that flares up again it'd be proper nasty because it'd wouldn't be swords and stuff, it'd be drones and nukes.'

Anyway, that's the backstory. I keep referring to Candy's mum and dad but Candy hadn't even been born at this stage of the story.

Eventually, she popped out, so tiny and precious, into a world that was so big and scary. They loved Candy so much that they vowed to protect her from danger.

All danger. Always.

Everything was going swimmingly until their little girl was 6. She was playing outside when she fell and grazed her knee. She wandered in from the garden, her bottom lip wobbling, a little bit of blood dribbling down her shin.

'Oh my goodness, Princess Candy,' said her mum. 'What has that nasty garden done to you?'

The little girl was scooped up, hugged, her knee sorted, dinosaur Elastoplast applied, crying stopped... job done.

Except, not quite. Candy's grazed knee wasn't the end of the matter. In fact it was the just beginning. Her mum and dad were determined that the big bad world wouldn't do any more harm to their precious little princess.

It all got a little out of hand. Let me explain.

Age 7, Candy wanted to play football. 'Ooh, that's dangerous,' said her dad. 'I watched some football on the TV and they kicked each other. There was tripping too. One man fell over and rolled around like he was badly hurt. And if the ball hits your head you get Alzheimer's.'

So Candy got wrapped in cotton wool. Literally. Her dad went to the chemist and cleared the entire shelf. He bought three trolleys of cotton wool, and rolls and rolls of Sellotape and he wrapped Candy up.

It was difficult to play football, but she tried her best. Eventually she got too hot and gave up. Her dad un-cottonwooled her. 'Excellent,' he said, inspecting her knees and elbows, 'no damage done.'

Age 8, Candy asked her mum, 'Is it okay if I have some swimming lessons?'

Her mum looked horrified. 'Swimming?' she gawped, 'in a pool. Made entirely of water!' Her mum shivered at the thought. 'What if you drown?'

So the very next day dad arranged for the plug to be pulled and the swimming pool to be emptied. They watched as the water glug glugged away and then Candy was allowed in. She had a lesson, splashing around in the dryness, front crawling in the fresh air, breast-stroke walking into the deep end. Mum and dad looked at each other, pleased as punch. 'Look at our little girl in the deep end, on her very first lesson!'

On the way home Candy commented that her swimming lesson had been, and I quote, 'weird and not much fun'.

'But at least you didn't drown,' smiled mum.

Age 9 and Candy hardly dared to ask, but she eventually plucked up the courage at teatime; 'Mum, you know that tall tree in the garden. Do you think I could climb it?'

Dad nearly choked on his jacket potato. Mum looked very worried. 'It's such a tall tree,' she said. 'What if you fell down. Or got to the top and couldn't climb down. You'd be stuck there forever, and die.'

Dad chipped in, his domino thinking in overdrive. 'Or if you got to the top and there was a storm, with lightning. It could strike the tree and that'd be worse than terrible.'

But Candy really wanted to climb the tree so, that night, mum and dad had a secret discussion and the next day Candy awoke, opened her curtains and - ta-daaaa – the tree had been chopped down. Yes, her loving father had been up all night chop chop chopping and then cutting all the sharpest branches off so that his little princess could climb the tree.

Safely!

He sure did love his little princess.

Candy climbed the tree. It was a bit boring but at least she was safe.

Age 10. Candy had seen some of the other children playing on a play-ground in the local park. She'd given up asking because she knew the slide would be too slippery, the swings too swingy and the climbing frame too fally-downy. But there was one piece of equipment that looked epic so that night, after tea, she put her Princess Candy eyes on and said, 'Daddy, would it be okay if I had a bounce on a trampoline?'

Her dad winced. He imagined all the things that could go wrong with a trampoline. Falling off and hurting yourself was the most obvious danger but all that bouncing might make his daughter sick, or she might pull a muscle, or she might bounce so high that she she'd be hit by a plane. He looked at those pleading eyes and decided he'd make his little princess a safe trampoline.

He got some cushions from the lounge and put them on the back lawn. Candy was allowed to jump up and down on the cushions for as long as she wanted.

Which wasn't very long.

It wasn't nearly as fun as an actual trampoline, in fact it was hardly any fun at all, but at least she was safe. 'And that's the main thing,' beamed dad.

Look here dear reader, I think you've got the point. The pattern was set.

Age 11, roller skating… no wheels.

Age 12, rugby… she was allowed to watch it on telly.

Age 13, horse riding… on a rocking horse.

Age 14, cooking… nothing hot or sharp, so she was allowed to peel a banana.

Age 15, art and design… no glue or scissors.

Age 16, exams… what if she failed and felt bad? To avoid feelings of disappointment, Candy was removed from exams.

These are just a few examples of what happened to Candy when she was a child. But, as happens to us all, eventually she became an adult, then middle aged, then old, then really old, then ancient.

Ancient Candy sat in her chair. She'd lived a very safe and long life. Her great grandchildren visited her in the nursing home. Lulu scrambled up onto Candy's bony knee. 'Tell me about the adventures you had growing up, Great Grandma,' she asked.

'Adventures?' asked her Great Grandma.

'Yes, you know, games and fun and stuff,' beamed tiny Lulu. 'Expeeeeeriences!'

Great Grandma Candy sat back in her chair, tears welling in her ancient eyes.

Thinking Aloud

1 It's said that old people rarely regret the things they did. Indeed, their biggest regrets are often about things they *didn't* do. What are your thoughts on this?

2 There's a well-known saying that 'life's a contact sport'. How much contact are you willing to expose yourself to?

3 What are the implications of too much risk?

4 What are the implications of too little risk?

5 When you're as old as Great Grandma Candy, what would a 'no regrets' life look like?

A WINDOW ON THE WORLD

A young couple moved into a swanky apartment in a new neighbourhood. They sat in their kitchen having breakfast, watching the world go by. The woman saw her neighbour pegging out the washing. 'That laundry's not very clean,' she tutted. 'She either needs a new washing machine or better washing powder.'

Other than the crunching on his toast, her husband remained silent.

His wife's comment was exactly the same the next day. And the next. 'Why on earth is that woman hanging out *dirty* washing?' she sighed in disgust. 'She needs lessons in basic hygiene!'

And her husband crunched, knowingly.

On the fourth day his wife plonked herself at the breakfast table with a gleeful smile. 'At last,' she said, pointing at their neighbour's washing line.' Her husband followed her gaze to the neatly arranged clothes line where the whites sparkled and the colours shone. 'All of a sudden she seems to have learned to clean properly.'

And her husband broke his silence. 'I got up early this morning and cleaned our windows.'

Something to Help Clear Your Thinking . . .

This isn't even original. I've read it somewhere before. It's just a silly story about a grumpy wife and a bloke washing the windows.

True or false?

Explain.

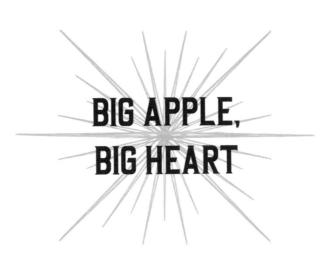

BIG APPLE, BIG HEART

What do you think of when I say 'New York cabbie'? Go ahead, stereotype away!

I'm guessing big yellow taxi, an iconic way of travelling in the Big Apple and probably stressed-out drivers who can be a bit rude.

That last stereotype comes from the demands of the job. We're in NYC traffic 12 hours a day. Our passengers are often in a rush to catch a plane, get to the theatre or they're late for a meeting. It's unfortunate but, as cabbies, our customers often look down on us. The pay ain't great. If the customer starts on about politics or the weather or the queues, we'll be sure to weigh in with our opinion. All right already!

I've been taxiing in NYC for 14 years. I've seen and heard it all. But here's the story of a fare that changed my life 3 years ago.

Buckle up and enjoy the ride.

I arrived at my last call of what had been a very busy shift.

This was back in the day, pre-Uber. There was no app to tell the customer you'd arrived so I did what cabbies did back then: I honked the horn.

After waiting two minutes I honked again. Come on, come on, lady. I was exhausted. Since this was going to be the last ride of my shift I thought about just driving away, but instead I put the car in park, walked up to the door and knocked. 'Just a minute', answered a frail, elderly voice. After a long pause, the door opened. A small woman in her 80s – maybe even her 90s – stood before me. She was wearing a print dress and a pillbox hat with a veil pinned on it, like somebody out of an Agatha Christie movie. By her side was a small suitcase.

'Would you be able to help me with my suitcase?' she smiled. 'It's a little on the heavy side.'

I entered her apartment and grabbed the bag. Heavy for her maybe, but for a burly New York cabbie, it was a piece of cake. I noticed all the furniture was covered with sheets and the walls and shelves were bare. In the corner was a cardboard box filled with photos and glassware. The old lady wasn't going on holiday, she was moving out.

All exhausted cabbies know that they like the last call of the day to be a straightforward affair; quick, easy, with a generous tip. This one was shaping to be the opposite, but I have an elderly mother and, contrary to the movie stereotype, we New Yorkers can do empathy.

I took the suitcase to the cab, then returned to assist the woman. She took my arm and we walked slowly toward the curb. Painfully slowly I might add. She kept thanking me for my kindness. 'It's nothing,' I told her. 'I just try to treat my passengers the way I would want my mom to be treated.' That was a half-truth. The full truth is that I provide extraordinary service if you catch me on a good day, otherwise the pressures of city traffic, impatient customers and low wages grind me down and my service might seem a little surly.

Anyhow, when we got in the cab, she gave me an address and then asked, 'Could you drive through downtown?'

'It's not the shortest way, ma'am,' I answered, my eye on the clock, noticing that my shift officially finished 3 minutes ago.

'Oh, I don't mind,' she said. 'I'm in no hurry. I'm on my way to a hospice.'

Cue a very long sigh from me. I looked in the rear-view mirror. Her eyes were glistening. Mine too, to be fair. 'I don't have any family left,' she continued in a soft voice. 'The doctor says I don't have very long.'

Note, my sigh wasn't an impatient huff, more of a 'do the right thing' intake and outtake of breath. I quietly reached over and shut off the meter. Again, not with a heavy heart, but with a kind one. 'What route would you like me to take?' I asked.

For the next two hours, we drove through the city. The other Big Apple drivers were their usual rushed and impatient selves, but not me. It was more of a cruise. She showed me the building where she had once worked as an elevator operator. Imagine, back in the day that was a genuine job! We drove through the neighbourhood where she and her late husband had lived when they were newlyweds. She had me pull up in front of a furniture warehouse that had once been a ballroom where she had gone dancing as a girl. She smiled as she told me that her husband had asked her to dance, in that very furniture showroom, almost 70 years ago. Sometimes she'd ask me to slow in front of a particular building or corner and would sit in the back seat just watching the neighbourhood unfold, saying nothing.

Then, all of a sudden, I heard, 'It's okay to go now'.

We drove in silence to the address she had given me. It was a low building, a small convalescent home, with a driveway that passed under a portico. Two orderlies came out to the cab as soon as we pulled up. I opened the trunk and took the small suitcase to the door. The woman was already seated in a wheelchair. 'How much do I owe you?' she asked, reaching into her purse.

'Nothing,' I said. 'You've given me a unique tour of New York. I've been to places I've never seen before. I should be paying you,' I smiled.

'You have to make a living,' she answered.

'There are other passengers,' I responded and almost without thinking, I bent and gave her a hug. She held onto me ever so tightly.

'You gave an old woman a little moment of joy,' she said. 'Thank you.'

I squeezed her hand, and then walked back to my cab. Behind me, a door shut. It was the sound of the closing of a life.

The Reflection Begins Where the Journey Ends

The story is powerful enough to leave right there. You'll have your own thoughts and feelings about what you've just read. While you mull it over, it's worth reading the reflection of the taxi driver himself. In his own words…

'I drove home, lost in thought. For the rest of the evening, I could hardly talk. What if that woman had gotten an angry driver, or one who was impatient to end his shift? What if that angry driver had been me? What if I had refused to take the run, or had honked once, then driven away?

'After mulling it over for the hundredth time, I don't think I have done anything more important in my life than give that lady a final look at her city.

'We're conditioned to think that our lives revolve around great moments. But great moments often catch us unaware – beautifully wrapped in what others may consider a small one. An extraordinary moment was hiding in an ordinary day. And while I can't afford to offer free rides to every customer, I can offer world-class service to every customer.

'I figure the world is very good at making passengers feel hurried. They're always in a rush. I guess that's why they're sometimes a bit rude. My job has always been to get them from A to B. The difference is that nowadays, every passenger gets a smile and a *positive* conversation.

'*Every* passenger. *Every* time.'

UBER UNCOOL

*Never worry what cool
people think.
Head for the warm people.
Life is warmth.
You'll be cool when you're
dead.
[Matt Haig]*

There was a teenager – let's call him Robbie – who was nice-but-not-cool. In fact he was *super*-nice-but-not-cool. The thing about Robbie is that he wasn't worried about being cool. It's not that he didn't care, more that he couldn't be bothered with how others preened and painted and hand-crafted their look. Robbie cared about other things. He was one of those kids who went under the radar. He had a handful of besties and everyone else in the school liked him – but didn't know much about him. There must have been something fishy about his home life because Robbie missed a lot of lessons, which frustrated the teachers.

His un-coolness centred on two things; his hair and his trousers. Robbie was self-aware. He knew about both. And yet he didn't change either [which, plot spoiler alert, made him kind of cool]

His hair was hit and miss. Robbie's hair came in phases. Occasionally it was good, but mostly bad. And by 'bad' I mean thin, blonde and unstylish. In fact, on a really bad hair day he wore a hat. Yes, all day at school he sometimes wore a beanie because the beanie was actually cooler than his actual hair.

And, worse still, his mum ironed creases into his school trousers. It got Robbie 'bullied' a bit in year 8 with 'bullied' in inverted commas because nobody pushed or shoved him around, but there were sniggers as he got on the school bus. Creased trousers gave Robbie a geeky look. 'Those creases dude, you're too school for cool.'

Robbie smiled and nodded. Like I said, he didn't really care.

You get the picture. Thoroughly nice lad but with inconsistent hair and bad trousers. And too many days off. That was Robbie.

And then, age 15, Robbie stopped coming to school at all. His leukaemia had finally got the better of him.

And, do you know what, when it was announced in assembly, it turned out that hardly anyone in school even knew he had blood cancer. He'd never announced it, never used it as an excuse for late homework, never complained about feeling dire and never skipped a PE lesson because of it. Robbie had just done what Robbie did. He'd showed up, poorly as hell, and done his level best.

After the funeral, his besties organised a Robbie Memorial Day, a charity fundraiser, all proceeds to cancer research. They raised £882.06. It was non-uniform and, guess what, every single kid rocked up with a woolly hat and creases ironed into their jeans.

Back to Skool

Yes, it's an allegory. Robbie's story **IS** the message. *Which is?*

THE GRAPES
OF WRATH

When my grandad reached the ripe old age of 92, he became poorly. I sat by his hospital bed for an entire day, hoping and praying that the old man would pull through. His lungs weren't working properly, which sounds pretty bad but, believe it or not, his biggest concern was that he hadn't had a poo for six days.

Imagine!

SIX whole days!

'Gosh grandad,' I said, 'when it does come it's gonna be an elephant turd.'

He managed a smile but when you're really poorly nothing is very funny. And while I sat, the old man kept getting visitors. Family and friends would rock up and grandad accumulated the world's biggest stash of grapes. (What is it about ill people and grapes?)

Anyhow, visitor after visitor visited and they all did *exactly* the same thing. They appeared through the door, took one look at the frail 92 year old, attempted a watery smile and then said, 'Oh my goodness, George, you look terrible,' followed by, 'How are you feeling?'

To be clear, 100% of the grape-carrying clan said the exact same thing: 'You look terrible' (which is a bad start to any conversation) followed by 'How are you feeling?' (which is a really awful follow-up question for hospital patients). Remember, he's a 92-year-old man whose lungs aren't working, clinging onto life in a hospital ward, and he hasn't had a poo in **SIX** whole days.

And yet they **ALL** asked, 'How are you feeling?'

HOW ARE YOU FEELING?

After the 8th time, I started to get irritated. I wanted to answer on my grandad's behalf. 'How do you think I'm chuffin' well feeling? I'm 92 for goodness' sake. I'm in hospital. I'm dehydrated. I've got tubes sticking out of my arms and this oxygen thingy up my nose. My lungs have stopped inflating which, to be fair, is never good news. I've been poked and prodded by the doctors. I'm on all sorts of pills and drugs. The food's rubbish. The bloke in the next bed keeps shouting in the night so I've had no sleep. I'm wired to a machine that keeps bleeping and if that bleep stops, it's game over. I'm hanging onto life. I've never felt worse. I've not had a poo since last Tuesday. I feel bloody awful. Oh, and by the way, **I HATE** grapes!'

Of course, my grandad was too polite to say any of that so he'd whisper through the driest of lips, 'Oh, you know, surviving.'

I became worried. 'Gosh, you look awful' followed by 'How are you feeling?' was a double-barrelled negative. The people meant well but those questions were actually making my grandad worse. The very old man, forever the life and soul of all our lives, was losing his life and soul. Visitors number eight left, so I decided to mix it up. I let the old chap have a sleep and I waited at the door to intercept batch nine. It happened to be Aunty Ella and Uncle Stan. I confiscated their grapes and whisked them away to the hospital café to brief them on my cunning plan.

A *resuscitation* plan.

I resumed my place next to grandad and 5 minutes later Aunty Ella and Uncle Stan burst through the door, huge smiles on their faces. Aunty Ella said, 'Gosh George, we went to the shop and they were all out of grapes so we've bought you this,' she said holding out the biggest bar of chocolate that my grandad had ever seen.

'No grapes!' smiled grandad, perking up a little. I thought I saw a twinkle in his eye.

'And on the way here,' gushed Uncle Stan, 'we got chatting about some of the holidays we used to have. You know, back in the day. When we all used to go away to the seaside. We couldn't decide which was our favourite. Ella says Llandudno. That year when about 20 of us went and you and me went skinny dipping. But I'm like, that was a goodun, Ella, but remember the coach trip to the illuminations in '81? Anyhow, we thought you could settle it for us. What's the best holiday you can remember George?'

And, oh my word, I watched through a teary eye as my grandad sat up, perked up and wouldn't shut up, as the three of them chatted excitedly about their best holiday memories.

My aunty and uncle left an hour later. The world's biggest bar of chocolate had been demolished by three old age pensioners. My grandad had laughed so hard that the tube came out of his nose. The nurses had actually asked them to shush because their laughter was keeping the shouting man awake.

My grandad had totally forgotten he was ill. In fact, I think he'd totally forgotten he was 92. Best of all, all that laughing had shaken his body up because as I got up to leave and kissed him on the forehead he had a huge smile etched on his face as he whispered, 'On your way out can you ask the nurse to pop by. I need a poo.'

An Argument is Brewing...

Two authors, one book.

There comes a point where we need to decide which content is in and which is left on the cutting room floor. It can get tense.

Here's a snippet of a behind the scenes conversation about 'The grapes of wrath'...

DR ANDY:	'Mate, I can live with story about 'Robbie', the ill teenager, but that nonsense about grandad not being able to poo. That's gotta go.'

PROF PAUL [CRESTFALLEN]:	'It's a keeper. It's not about grandad's bowel movements.'
DR ANDY:	'It is. It says he's not been to the loo for 6 whole days and then, in the end, he managed one.'
PROF PAUL [RAISING HIS VOICE, WHICH IS RARE]:	'It's **NOT** about how to solve constipation. It's a very subtle take on something much deeper than that.'
DR ANDY [SOUNDING SCEPTICAL]:	'Deeper than constipation? Well if it's not about toilet habits what is it about?'

PLEASE COMPLETE PAUL'S ANSWER IN LESS THAN 30 WORDS:

_____

_____

_____

_____

_____

RENTING OR OWNING?

Picking your rental car up from the airport is *never* a joyful experience. Never *ever!*

Despite having ticked all the boxes online, there's still a wad of paperwork to sign at the desk, plus the obligatory sales pitch about extra insurance. By the time they've converted the online price from pounds to euros to bitcoin and back again, it's somehow mushroomed into a much bigger number than you were expecting. Rather conveniently for them, they don't speak quite enough English and you have zero Spanish, so you sigh and sign.

You trundle your luggage across the vast car park. You clickety clack past Hertz, Europcar, Avis, Alamo, Sixt and all the other well-known brands that you couldn't afford, until you finally arrive at DirtCheapCarsRUs, heave your luggage into the tiny boot and familiarise yourself with the existing dents and scratches. Satisfied that there are too many to count you adjust the seat and mirrors. Religious people will then do the sign of the cross, the non-religious will take a deep breath, and you pull away onto the wrong side of the road.

Five minutes later your confidence is back on an even keel. You've navigated your first roundabout and apart from accidentally putting the windscreen wipers on when you wanted to turn left, you're pretty much unscathed. You find yourself cruising at 120 km/hr in a 100 zone, wondering what that is in British speed.

A week later, holiday over, you return to the airport. You thought you had plenty of time but 45 minutes disappeared while you went on a detour to find a petrol station. Slightly stressed, you pull up at DirtCheapCarsRUs, wait nervously while someone with a clipboard inspects for new scratches and/or dents, before getting the thumbs-up to go join a 200 m check-in queue.

Questions: how did you treat the car, and did you wash and vacuum it before you returned it to the airport?

I'm guessing your answers are 'shabbily' and 'of course I bloody well didn't', respectively.

You might have accelerated faster and braked harder than at home. Your rental probably had a smaller engine than you're used to so your foot-to-the-floor policy was needed to get her up to speed. There might have been some accidental damage. The lack of respect for your car is because you were renting and, of course, cleaning the vehicle is DirtCheapCarsRUs's responsibility.

Hey, it's an allegory, so you'll have to work out the true meaning for yourself.

Here's a clue. Your body is your means of transport. It gets you through life. Our question is simply this: are you renting or owning?

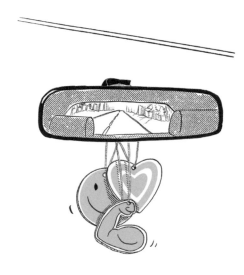

THE FLUFFY TALE
OF BABBITY RABBIT

Now you don't see it.
Now you do!

Once upon a time there was a little girl called Sophie. She was 3 years old.

She had dozens of cuddly toys and she loved them all, but there was one, a rabbity thing, that was her absolute favourite. The rabbity thing was actually older than she was. It had been purchased by her grandma and placed in her Moses basket, awaiting baby Sophie's arrival.

All the way to 5 months, baby Sophie dribbled and sucked on the rabbity thing. Then she learned to talk baby-babble and she had pretend conversations with the rabbit thing until, at age 11 months, and to her mum's absolute dismay, 'Babbit' had been the little girl's first word.

So 'Mr Babbit' is what the rabbity thing became.

Sophie and Mr Babbit were inseparable. They had tea parties together. Mr Babbit could be seen poking out of the top of Sophie's backpack as she walked to nursery. Mr Babbit got pride of place next to little Sophie at bedtime. Each night, after the bedtime story was finished, daddy would close the book, kiss his daughter on the forehead and tuck her in. Then the little girl would wriggle with love as Mr Babbit was tucked in beside her.

Daddy would leave the room, switching the light off as he went but because he was a very good Daddy he'd be sure to keep the door ajar so there was a little bit of light.

And that's how it went, night after night after night. Little Sophie would fall asleep, happy and comforted, knowing that Mr Babbit was beside her, making her feel safe, snuggly and all loved up.

Night after night after night…

After night after night…

After night.

Until, all of a sudden, Sophie was 21 years and one day old. The young woman's alarm went off and it was adult o'clock. She stretched and opened her bleary eyes. Sophie's head was throbbing and her mouth tasted like a sewer. The following memories are blurry because there was a party involved. A special coming-of-age one and, on reflection, Sophie had definitely drunk more than she should.

The start of yesterday was easy to remember. There were lots of prezzies, a glass of something bubbly and a Skype from the care home where her great grandma lived. Those chats were always funny because you could only ever see great grandma's eye or left ear, and she shouted on Skype.

I think she thought that's how it worked.

Sophie remembered the first pub and the absolute hilarity. She remembered the buzz of a party mid flow. She remembered laughing until her face ached. She recalled a lovely atmosphere where her school and uni friends all mingled together, her dad said a few teary words about his 'favourite baby girl', Aunty Lily did her funny dancing, Brendan tapped off with Guy (this time it looked serious!) and...

Sophie sat bolt upright in bed...

Mr Babbit!

Sophie remembered that Lizzie had found Mr Babbit in her bag and he got passed around the pub. Jack made him pretend to drink beer. Which, to be fair, was very funny. Then Mr Babbit was made to eat some peanuts and poo them out again. Jack again, I think? Again, funny.

Mr Babbit came with them to the next pub and, on the way, the boys played rugby with him. Matty had thrown Mr Babbit to Josh, and then to Raj, but everyone was a bit tiddly and Mr Babbit had landed in the road.

Sophie's head throbbed as she relived the agony of what happened next. She remembered squealing as a car squished Mr Babbit. It was a busy road so nobody could rescue the little creature and by the time Matty had dashed to recover Mr Babbit he'd been run over by two lorries, a bus, several cars and, somewhat ironically, an actual ambulance.

It's strange what alcohol can do. It heightens your emotions so, as a sober 21 year old Sophie would have laughed at the squashed cuddly toy, but the tipsy Sophie was teary. The body of squished Mr Babbit had been put in a plastic bag and the party girl sobbed for a whole hour until Rhianna promised, a little drunkenly, there would be a Mr Babbit funeral and that they'd all pay their respects.

Sophie vaguely remembered somebody proposing a toast to Mr Babbit. She couldn't remember the exact words. 'RIP Mr Babbit. Ashes to ashes, funk to funky, Major Tom and all that. May the force be with you.' They'd all raised their glasses. That had made her smile through her sniffles.

Whatever. It was hazy.

Sophie swung her legs out of bed, the effort making her head pound some more. She looked at last night's rucksack, the plastic bag poking out. She removed the bag, put her hand inside and felt the furry rabbit thing. She clutched her lifetime companion and pulled him out.

Oh my goodness! Mr Babbit was squashed alright. The busy A417 hadn't been kind. Sophie examined her cuddly friend. He had tyre marks across his body and a drop of oil on his head. Worse still, the seam on his tummy had ripped open and his Babbity guts were hanging out. She took some of the stuffing and tried to re-stuff it back inside, which is when she noticed something amazing.

Something amazingly simple, that is.

So amazingly simple that you'll have already worked it out. Mr Babbit was made of cloth. His eyes were black beads, his nose was stitching and his innards were made of foam.

Let me say that last bit again, because it's such a huge point. **HIS INNARDS WERE MADE OF FOAM!**

Sophie's companion of twenty one years (and a day) had been making her feel comforted, safe and loved, and yet he contained no love.

He contained stuffing.

Sophie could feel the blood pounding in her temples. She remembered one traumatic night, many years ago, when daddy had read the bedtime story and Mr Babbit had gone missing. Sophie remembered the trauma and tears lasting a whole hour before Mr Babbit had been found in the car. As soon as he was tucked up in bed beside her, her sobbing had stopped. Mr Babbit had made her feel happy, safe and loved.

And I mean it *reaaaaaally* seemed as though the feelings were coming from the rabbit. She furrowed her brow and thought as hard as her hangover would allow:

No Mr Babbit = panic and tears.

Finding Mr Babbit = happiness and love.

But here she was, staring at the proof. Mr Babbit's guts were leaking out and he contained no love.

Not even 1% love.

He was 100% stuffing

Sophie's insight was that 100% of those feelings – love, comfort, safety and happiness – must have been totally coming from within her.

That's weird, thought grown-up Sophie. Her head was now throbbing with insight rather than alcohol. She realised that as an adult she was doing exactly the same. She'd moved on from cuddly toys but instead was attaching her emotions to more grown-up things and she'd been hook, line and sinkered into thinking her feelings were coming to her from uni assignments, someone un-liking her on social media, her mum nagging her, her little brother annoying her, her new haircut, the presentation she was having to give next week, a hug from her boyfriend, a bad hair day, a good hair day, a rainy Monday, a sunny Wednesday, 3.30 on Friday…

Whereas the truth is that feelings are always generated from within.

Sophie'd had a blinding flash of the bleedin' obvious: she realised it wasn't just her. It's how all human beings work. Nobody is feeling the outside world, we are all feeling our thinking.

Sophie took squished Mr Babbit and decided to go back to bed. Her headache had evaporated. Her thinking had never been clearer.

She pulled the duvet up to her chin and snuggled up beside her beloved toy and poked a bit more of his innards back where they should be.

Sophie had experienced a massive whoosh of understanding. She totally 'got' the nature of inside-out thinking and realised it would change everything but, gosh, it was going to be super-tricky to explain this to anyone else because although it kind of makes perfect sense, the world is very good at making you think the total opposite. Just as 21-year-old Sophie would have sworn blind that Mr Babbit was making her feel safe, she realised that people would swear double blind that their feelings are coming from the outside world. And, she realised, if you think that, you will spend your entire life getting upset about things that are happening to you.

She said it out loud to herself, just to make sure it still made sense; 'I am not feeling the outside world, I am feeling my thinking.'

Sophie had seen the news. She was well aware that the world's far from perfect. And when you have angry and upsetting thoughts… that's what you'll end up feeling!

Sophie twigged that the previous generation has handed her global warming and oceans of plastic to deal with. And at an individual level she had exams, student debt and a property ladder with a ridiculously high first rung. The media loved to prod her with a stick and provoke some irritation, causing Sophie to think negative thoughts…

…and all of a sudden everything fell into place.

If every feeling I ever experience is coming from my thinking, and my thinking is mostly negative…

… anger, frustration, anxiety, worry, panic, a sense of being on edge – it's not what's going on around me, it's what's going on *inside* me.

Emotions work from the inside out!

Sophie realised this is a complete reversal of how life appears to you but it is, nevertheless, the way you operate. You are, in fact, feeling your thinking in this moment.

Always!

For Sophie, it was the 'always' bit that was the most amazing piece of the realisation jigsaw. You can never have a feeling without first having a thought. (If you're anything like Sophie, you'll have to let that fact settle for a wee while.)

She lay there trying to pick holes in her new theory. *I'm nervous about my final exams next month, she thought. Or at least it sure feels that way.*

She wrinkled her nose and looked at Mr Babbit for inspiration. 'How can I be feeling nervous about an exam that's not even here yet?' she asked her toy. 'That's ridiculous! How does the feeling of nervousness about an exam next month reach me in this moment?'

She smiled at Mr Babbit. 'Oh my gosh Babs, my feelings of nervousness, the ones I'm feeling right now, aren't coming from next month's exams. They're coming from me thinking about next month's exams. My feelings are totally coming from whatever I'm thinking *in this moment*.'

She lay there and pondered a dozen situations and it was the exact same answer a dozen times.

Anyway, you can't lie in bed all day pondering the meaning of life, so the time came when the young woman had to get out of bed, grab a shower, get dressed, and crack on. A strong black coffee awaited!

The next 6 months were a bit weird. Nothing had changed, and yet everything had changed. As Sophie became more immersed in inside-out thinking, outside influences started to cause less of a stink. She was a whole lot calmer. The weight of the world she'd been shouldering, it was gone.

In case you're wondering, she smashed her exams, by the way.

Life's wasn't perfect and she sometimes forgot but, overall, life felt lighter. As a result, Sophie began enjoying it a whole lot more. Sure, one of her uni lecturers was still be a bit of an idiot, the assignment workload was still unfair, the sun didn't always shine, trolls continued to create anti-social media, her little brother was still not perfect, her mum sometimes nagged, she still had to go and visit her gran, her student loan still didn't cover her outgoings… but their power to upset Sophie has gone.

She was free!

She started to notice that most people weren't free. They continued to think worried thoughts and, as a result, carried anxiety with them. This was another **OH MY GOSH** moment. *They're carrying it with them.* Sophie realised anxiety wasn't about people's circumstances, it was about their thinking.

Of course, it really looks as though it's their circumstances and if you ask them, they'll absolutely think it is. Lottie was anxious about getting a job, Stav twitchy about his grades, Cindy was stressed out about money, Fi about her weight, Dylan about his poorly mum, Dev was anxious about pretty much everything…

And yet none of it was true. Everyone was worrying themselves sick. *Literally!* Dev was on worry pills!

Sophie's inside-out thinking meant she was able to do the opposite: *un-worry* herself well.

The young woman felt clearer of mind because she had less on it! She felt less stress, less anxiety, less anger and had fewer arguments. Her biggest **AHA** moment was Mondays.

Yes, actual Mondays!

She was a bit embarrassed when she realised she'd accidentally learned to hate them. In fact, she'd pretty much wasted a seventh of her entire life because she's learned to think about Mondays in a negative way. She'd looked around at everyone else and they hated Mondays, so she'd just joined in. And yet, in reality, it had never been about Mondays. For 21 years (and one day), it'd always been how she was *thinking* about Mondays.

So she re-thought Mondays. I mean, it's not actually that hard to do. Monday was an opportunity to kick-start her week in a positive fashion. Monday was an opportunity to bring some energy and happiness to her lecturers, family and friends. Monday was an opportunity to shine.

So she did.

And when you learn to shine, good things happen to you so, rest assured, this is a happily ever after story. The young woman learned to cease trying to mould the world to fit what she wanted it to be, and began to accept it for how it was. It was a bit spooky but as she fixed her thinking, she found that she accidentally fixed herself.

Oh, and by the way, Sophie also fixed Mr Babbit. She gave him bright red cross stitch down his tummy to remind her about inside-out thinking. She continued to cuddle him every night, safe in the knowledge that her loving thoughts were creating her loved up feeling.

Thank you, you lovely snuggly Babbity thing.

Turning Your Thinking Inside-Out

1 Go grab one of your kid's cuddly toys. Slice it open. We're curious. Let us know if there's any love inside. Or it is just stuffing?

2 What adult 'Mr Babbits' do you have in your life? What objects, people or situations are you hanging your emotions on?

3 What would be the benefits of realising that your feelings are coming from your thinking *in this moment?*

4 Let the learning settle and report back using #MrBabbit.

More books by *Andy Cope* and *Paul McGee*

ANDY COPE

The Art of Being Brilliant: Transform Your Life by Doing What Works for You
Andy Cope and Andy Whittaker
9780857083715

Be Brilliant Every Day
Andy Cope and Andy Whittaker
9780857085009

The Art of Being a Brilliant Teenager
Andy Cope, Andy Whittaker, Darrell Woodman and Amy Bradley
9780857085788

Shine: Rediscovering Your Energy, Happiness and Purpose
Andy Cope and Gavin Oattes
9780857087652

Diary of a Brilliant Kid: Top Secret Guide to Awesomeness
Andy Cope, Gavin Oattes and Will Hussey
9780857087867

The Little Book of Being Brilliant
Andy Cope
9780857087973

Zest: How to Squeeze the Max out of Life
Andy Cope, Gavin Oattes and Will Hussey
9780857088000

How to Be a Well Being: Unofficial Rules to Live Every Day
Andy Cope, Sanjeev Sandhu and James Pouliopoulos
9780857088673

A Girl's Guide to Being Fearless: How to Find Your Brave
Suzie Lavington and Andy Cope
9780857088574

PAUL McGEE

S.U.M.O. (Shut Up, Move On): The Straight-Talking Guide to Succeeding in Life,
10th Anniversary Edition
Paul McGee
9780857086228

SUMO your Relationships: How to Handle Not Strangle the People You Live and Work With
Paul McGee
9781841127439

How Not to Worry: The Remarkable Truth of How a Small Change Can Help You Stress Less and Enjoy Life More
Paul McGee
9780857082862

How to Succeed with People: Remarkably Easy Ways to Engage, Influence and Motivate Almost Anyone
Paul McGee
9780857082893

How to Speak So People Really Listen: The Straight-Talking Guide to Communicating with Influence and Impact
Paul McGee
9780857087201

How to Have a Great Life: 35 Surprisingly Simple Ways to Success, Fulfilment and Happiness
Paul McGee
9780857087751

Self-confidence: The Remarkable Truth of How a Small Change Can Boost Your Resilience and Increase Your Success,
10th Anniversary Edition
Paul McGee
9780857088352

Yesss! The S.U.M.O. Secrets to Being a Positive, Confident Teenager
Paul McGee
9780857088710

About the Authors

Andy Cope is a qualified teacher, wellbeing expert and 'recovering academic'. His Loughborough University thesis was 12 years in the making, and the reward for grinding out his PhD is that Andy gets to call himself a 'Doctor of Happiness'. Don't worry – he's socially aware enough to understand that it's a terribly cheesy title, but a notch above the socially unacceptable alternative: 'Doctor Feelgood'.

Andy runs a training company that conducts keynotes and workshops all over the world. He has also developed a not-for-profit 'Brilliant Schools' project that aims to get positive psychology and wellbeing embedded into the curriculum.

He's an avid Derby County supporter, which provides some self-inflicted gloom in an otherwise epic life.

Business website: www.artofbrilliance.co.uk

School website: brilliant.school

Email: andy@artofbrilliance.co.uk

Twitter: @beingbrilliant

Insta: artofbrilliance

Paul McGee is a Sunday Times bestselling author, visiting Professor at The University of Chester and international keynote speaker – which is quite a surprise for someone with a background in banking and beefburgers.

Paul is proud creator of The SUMO (Shut Up, Move On) brand, a programme that is now used by organisations and schools throughout the world.

His Mum is an avid reader which may explain why he has sold over quarter of a million books to date.

His clients include the NHS, Manchester City Football Club, Adidas, GSK, Tesco, and several charities.

He combines his love of comedy and football by supporting both Wigan Athletic and Bradford City.

For more information go to:

Business website: www.theSUMOguy.com

School website: www.SUMO4Schools.com

Email: paul.mcgee@thesumoguy.com

Twitter: @thesumoguy

Insta: @thesumoguy

Index

L

Language, impact, 151–152, 157
Law of Accelerating Technology
(Moore), 33
Law of GOYA. *See* Get Off Your Ass
Leadership, discussion, 97
Learned behaviour, 60
Learned self, impact, 45
Life
audit, 81
boring life, 120
cab driver perspective, 215–219
change, 60
compare/contrast game, 133
contact sport, 211
events
influence, limitation, 119
occurrence, reason, 122
experience, impact, 80–81
fairness, absence, 117–118
game, 116–121
get-out clause, 113, 122
goal, 91
handling, 121
happiness by-product, 171–172
hatch, match, and dispatch, 190
lessons, learning, 121–123
lightness, 243
meaning, search, 89–90
metaphor, 132, 140
paradox, 37
passion, 195
plot twists, preparation, 194
proactive approach, 97
purpose, 87
satisfaction, improvement,
99
snake event, experience, 117
teenager perspective, 222–223

terms and conditions (Ts & Cs),
113–115, 117, 127
window, 213–214
Little Shop of Shame, 75, 81, 116
Lobotomy, usage, 53
Love
equation, 240
feeling, 169
promise, 196
tale, 235–245
Love tough, 79–80
Lower-order needs, domination,
139
Lucretius, 38
Lust, 175–178

M

Magic, creation, 142
Manic depression, 53
Man's Search for Meaning
(Frankl), 89
Marsden, Joy, 80
Materialism
escape, 173–174, 179
impact, 170
rental/ownership, decision,
231–233
Meaning
idea, demystification, 90
sense, requirement, 86–87, 89
Medications, availability, 58
Meditation, usage, 5
Mental bandwidth, increase
(requirement), 38
Mental fitness, impact, 64
Mental health, treatments, 52–53
Mental illness
health statistics, 22–23
pandemic, 22–23